DIRTIER LITTLE LIMERICKS

DIRTY & DIRTIER LITTLE LIMERICKS

Portland House
New York

This edition is published by Portland House, an imprint of
Random House Value Publishing, Inc., a division of Random House, Inc.
280 Park Avenue, New York, New York 10017.

Random House
New York • Toronto • London • Sydney • Auckland
http://www.randomhouse.com/

Printed and bound in the United States of America.

ISBN 0-517-48978-3

8 7 6 5 4 3 2 1

FOREWORD

Over three hundred fifty years ago Ben Jonson wrote a poem that began, "Doing a filthy business is." Poor old Ben, if he were around today, he would not have such a negative outlook. "Doing" may still not be the cleanest activity in the world, but it is surely fun. A healthier, more realistic attitude toward "doing" (or perhaps the discovery of penicillin) has led to an increased enjoyment of this pastime.

But if it is more fun to do it, it is also more fun to be naughty about it. The writers of limericks the five line poem, are unsurpassed in this skill. They are so good at being naughty that—well, let's face it—they are downright dirty. Dirty as opposed to filthy, of course. In this volume you will find *Dirty Little Limericks,* and although you may find it hard to imagine, we dug up some dirtier ones, in *Dirtier Little Limericks* and added them.

One is cheered that Edward Lear did not ruin a good literary genre and leave it stuck in the nursery. Although we know in our heart of hearts that the owl and the pussycat did more than dance by the light of the moon, such knowledge was never made public.

"Well," said the Wolf, "these six hundred eighty vivacious verses reveal things that Little Red Riding Hood's grandmother never dreamed of." Here you will be informed of Rosalina's ass, Scott and a twat, Miss Doves and her gloves, a wench who could do more than French, a man of Peru who had no one to screw, Jane with her cellophane—all these and more.

Yes, it is all here. And if you are overcome with shock at first, we predict that you will soon give way to a chuckle, then to a gusty guffaw.

DIRTY · LITTLE · LIMERICKS

LITTLE ROMANCES

❦

There was a young lady of Arden,
The tool of whose swain wouldn't harden.
    Said she with a frown,
  "I've been sadly let down
By the tool of a fool in a garden."

❦

There was a young girl in Berlin
Who was fucked by an elderly Finn.
    Though he diddled his best,
    And fucked her with zest,
She kept asking, "Hey, Pop, is it in?"

❦

I wooed a stewed nude in Bermuda,
I was lewd, but my God! she was lewder.
    She said it was crude
    To be wooed in the nude—
I pursued her, subdued her, and screwed her!

There was a young lady of Bicester
Who was nicer by far than her sister:
    The sister would giggle
    And wiggle and jiggle,
But this one would come if you kissed her.

❧

There was a young sailor from Brighton
Who remarked to his girl, "You're a tight one."
    She replied, "'Pon my soul,
    You're in the wrong hole;
There's plenty of room in the right one."

❧

A young woman got married at Chester,
Her mother she kissed and she blessed her.
    Says she, "You're in luck,
    He's a stunning good fuck,
For I've had him myself down in Leicester."

❧

A lady while dining at Crewe
Found an elephant's whang in her stew.
    Said the waiter, "Don't shout,
    And don't wave it about,
Or the others will all want one too."

There was a young lady of Dover
Whose passion was such that it drove her
To cry, when you came,
"Oh dear! What a shame!
Well, now we shall have to start over."

There was a young man of Dumfries
Who said to his girl, "If you please,
It would give me great bliss
If, while playing with this,
You would pay some attention to these!"

There was a young lady named Flynn
Who thought fornication a sin,
But when she was tight
It seemed quite all right,
So everyone filled her with gin.

There was a young fellow named Goody
Who claimed that he wouldn't, but would he?
If he found himself nude
With a gal in the mood,
The question's not woody but could he?

There was a young girl from Hong Kong
Who said, " You are utterly wrong
    To say my vagina
    's the largest in China,
Just because of your mean little dong."

❦

There was once a sad Maître d'hôtel
Who said, " They can all go to hell!
    What they do to my wife—
    Why it ruins my life;
And the worst is, they all do it well."

❦

There was a young man named Hughes
Who swore off all kinds of booze.
    He said, " When I'm muddled
    My senses get fuddled,
And I pass up too many screws."

❦

A pansy who lived in Khartoum
Took a lesbian up to his room,
    And they argued all night
    Over who had the right
To do what, and with which, and to whom.

There was an old lady who lay
With her legs wide apart in the hay,
    Then, calling the ploughman,
    She said, " Do it now, man!
Don't wait till your hair has turned gray. "

❧

There was a young plumber of Leigh
Who was plumbing a girl by the sea.
    She said, " Stop your plumbing,
    There's somebody coming! "
Said the plumber, still plumbing, " It's me. "

❧

There was a young fellow from Parma
Who was solemnly screwing his charmer.
    Said the damsel, demure,
  " You'll excuse me, I'm sure,
But I *must* say you fuck like a farmer. "

❧

There was a young man from Purdue
Who was only just learning to screw,
    But he hadn't the knack,
    And he got too far back—
In the right church, but in the wrong pew.

The king named Œdipus Rex
Who started this fuss about sex
    Put the world to great pains
    By the spots and the stains
Which he made on his mother's pubex.

❦

There was a young German named Ringer
Who was screwing an opera singer.
    Said he with a grin,
  " Well, I've sure got it in! "
Said she, " You mean that ain't your finger? "

❦

A young violinist from Rio
Was seducing a lady named Cleo.
    As she took down her panties
    She said, " No *andantes*;
I want this *allegro con brio!* "

❦

Said a lecherous fellow named Shea,
When his prick wouldn't rise for a lay,
  " You must seize it, and squeeze it,
    And tease it, and please it,
For Rome wasn't built in a day. "

There was a young man from Siam
Who said, "I go in with a wham,
    But I soon lose my starch
    Like the mad month of March,
And the lion comes out like a lamb."

❦

There was a young fellow named Skinner
Who took a young lady to dinner.
    At a quarter to nine
    They sat down to dine;
At twenty to ten it was in her.
    Skinner?
No, the dinner.

There was a young fellow named Tupper
Who took a young lady to supper.
    At a quarter to nine
    They sat down to dine,
And at twenty to ten it was up her.
    Tupper?
No, Skinner, the son of a bitch!

❦

"My back aches. My penis is sore.
I simply can't fuck any more.
    I'm dripping with sweat,
    And you haven't come yet;
And, my God! it's a quarter to four!"

There was a young lady of Spain
Who took down her pants on a train.
    There was a young porter
    Saw more than he orter,
And asked her to do it again.

❦

There once was a dentist named Stone
Who saw all his patients alone.
    In a fit of depravity
    He filled the wrong cavity,
And my, how his practice has grown!

❦

A sailor who slept in the sun
Woke to find his fly-buttons undone.
    He remarked with a smile,
  "Jesus Christ, a sundial!
And it's now a quarter past one."

❦

The spouse of a pretty young thing
Came home from the wars in the spring.
    He was lame but he came
    With his dame like a flame—
A discharge is a wonderful thing.

A pretty wife living in Tours
Demanded her daily amour.
    But the husband said, "No!
    It's too much. Let it go!
My backsides are dragging the floor."

❧

There was a young lady of Twickenham
Who thought men had not enough prick in 'em.
    On her knees every day
    To God she would pray
To lengthen and strengthen and thicken 'em.

❧

A couple was fishing near Clombe
When the maid began looking quite glum,
    And said, "Bother the fish!
    I'd rather coish!"
Which they did—which was why they had come.

❧

The limerick form is complex
Its contents run chiefly to sex.
    It burgeons with virgeons
    And masculine urgeons,
And swarms with erotic effex.

There was a young girl whose frigidity
Approached cataleptic rigidity
    Till you gave her a drink,
    When she quickly would sink
In a state of complaisant liquidity.

❦

There was a young fellow named Lancelot
Whom his neighbors all looked on askance a lot.
    Whenever he'd pass
    A presentable lass,
The front of his pants would advance a lot.

❦

There was a young student from Yale
Who was getting his first piece of tail.
    He shoved in his pole,
    But in the wrong hole,
And a voice from beneath yelled : "No sale!"

ORGANS

In the Garden of Eden lay Adam,
Complacently stroking his madam,
    And loud was his mirth
    For on all of the earth
There were only two balls—and he had 'em.

A chippy who worked in Black Bluff
Had a pussy as large as a muff.
    It had room for both hands
    And some intimate glands,
And was soft as a little duck's fluff.

There was a young fellow named Bowen
Whose pecker kept growin' and growin'.
    It grew so tremendous,
    So long and so pendulous,
'Twas no good for fuckin'—just showin'.

There was a young lady from Brussels
Who was proud of her vaginal muscles.
    She could easily plex them
    And so interflex them
As to whistle love songs through her bustles.

❦

There was a young girl of Cah'lina,
Had a very capricious vagina :
    To the shock of the fucker
    'Twould suddenly pucker,
And whistle the chorus of " Dinah ."

❦

A lady with features cherubic
Was famed for her area pubic.
    When they asked her its size
    She replied in surprise,
" Are you speaking of square feet, or cubic ? "

❦

There was a young fellow named Cribbs
Whose cock was so big it had ribs.
    They were inches apart,
    And to suck it took art,
While to fuck it took forty-two trips.

There was a young man from Hong Kong
Who had a trifurcated prong:
A small one for sucking,
A large one for fucking,
And a *honey* for beating a gong.

❧

A fellow whose surname was Hunt
Trained his cock to perform a slick stunt:
This versatile spout
Could be turned inside out,
Like a glove, and be used as a cunt.

❧

There was a young fellow named Kimble
Whose prick was exceedingly nimble,
But fragile and slender,
And dainty and tender,
So he kept it encased in a thimble.

❧

There was a young man of Madras
Whose balls were constructed of brass.
When jangled together
They played "Stormy Weather,"
And lightning shot out of his ass.

A bad little girl in Madrid,
A most reprehensible kid,
    Told her Tante Louise
    That her cunt smelled like cheese,
And the worst of it was that it did!

❦

There was a young man from Maine
Whose prick was as strong as a cane;
    It was almost as long,
    So he strolled with his dong
Extended in sunshine and rain.

❦

There was a young girl from Medina
Who could completely control her vagina.
    She could twist it around
    Like the cunts that are found
In Japan, Manchukuo and China.

❦

There was a young soldier from Munich
Whose penis hung down past his tunic,
    And their chops girls would lick
    When they thought of his prick,
But alas! he was only a eunuch.

There was a young lady of Natchez
Who chanced to be born with two snatches,
    And she often said, " Shit!
    Why, I'd give either tit
For a man with equipment that matches. "

❦

A girl of uncertain nativity
Had an ass of extreme sensitivity
    When she sat on the lap
    Of a German or Jap,
She could sense Fifth Column activity.

❦

There was a young fellow named Paul
Who confessed, " I have only one ball.
    But the size of my prick
    Is God's dirtiest trick,
For my girls always ask, 'Is that all?' "

❦

A young man from the banks of the Po
Found his cock had elongated so,
    That when he'd pee
    It was not he
But only his neighbors who'd know.

There was a fat man from Rangoon
Whose prick was much like a balloon.
    He tried hard to ride her
    And when finally inside her
She thought she was pregnant too soon.

❦

There was a young lady named Riddle
Who had an untouchable middle.
    She had many friends
    Because of her ends,
Since it isn't the middle you diddle.

❦

There was an old fellow named Skinner
Whose prick, his wife said, had grown thinner.
    But still, by and large,
    It would always discharge
Once he could just get it in her.

❦

There was a young lady from Spain
Whose face was exceedingly plain,
    But her cunt had a pucker
    That made the men fuck her,
Again, and again, and again.

There was a young man from Stamboul
Who boasted so torrid a tool
That each female crater
Explored by this satyr
Seemed almost unpleasantly cool.

❧

There was a young fellow of Strensall
Whose pecker was shaped like a pencil,
Anemic, 'tis true,
But an interesting screw,
Inasmuch as the tip was prehensile.

❧

A wonderful tribe are the Sweenies,
Renowned for the length of their peenies.
The hair on their balls
Sweeps the floors of their halls,
But they don't look at women, the meanies.

❧

There was an old man of Tagore
Whose tool was a yard long or more,
So he wore the damn thing
In a surgical sling
To keep it from wiping the floor.

There was a young man of Toulouse
Who had a deficient prepuce,
    But the foreskin he lacked
    He made up in his sac;
The result was, his balls were too loose.

❦

A cautious young fellow named Tunney
Had a whang that was worth any money.
    When eased in half-way,
    The girl's sigh made him say,
" Why the sigh? " " For the rest of it, honey. "

❦

A pious old woman named Tweak
Had taught her vagina to speak.
    It was frequently liable
    To quote from the Bible,
But when fucking—not even a squeak!

❦

When he tried to inject his huge whanger
A young man aroused his girl's anger.
    As they strove in the dark
    She was heard to remark,
" What you need is a zeppelin hangar. "

In the speech of his time, did the Bard
Refer to his prick as his "yard,"
    But sigh no more, madams:
    'Twas no longer than Adam's
Or mine, and not one half so hard.

❦

There was a young girl named Dalrymple
Whose sexual equipment was so simple
    That on examination they found
    Little more than a mound
In the center of which was a dimple.

❦

There was a young lady named Grace
Who had eyes in a very odd place.
    She could sit on the hole
    Of a mouse or a mole
And stare the beast square in the face.

❦

The nipples of Sarah Sarong,
When excited, are twelve inches long.
    This embarrassed her lover
    Who was pained to discover
She expected no less of his dong.

A damsel who lives at The Springs
Had her maidenhead ripped into strings
    By a hideous Kurd,
    And now, she averred,
" When the wind blows through it, it sings. "

❧

A Chinaman hailing from Wusih
Once laid an American floozie.
  " How different, " he cried,
    As he slid it inside,
" To diddle a vertical coozie! "

❧

There once was a young man named Lanny
The size of whose prick was uncanny.
    His wife, the poor dear,
    Took it into her ear,
And it came out the hole in her fanny.

❧

There once was an artist named Thayer
Who was really a cubist for fair.
    He looked all his life
    To find him a wife
Possessed of a cunt that was square.

There was a young squaw of Wohunt
Who possessed a collapsible cunt.
    It had many odd uses,
    Produced no papooses,
And fitted both giant and runt.

❦

There was a young laundress named Wrangle
Whose tits tilted up at an angle.
  " They may tickle my chin, "
    She said with a grin,
" But at least they keep out of the mangle. "

❦

STRANGE INTERCOURSE

❦

A young polo-player of Berkeley
Made love to his sweetheart berserkly.
    In the midst of each chukker
    He would break off and fuck her
Horizontally, laterally, and verkeley.

There was a young idler named Blood,
Made a fortune performing at stud,
    With a fifteen-inch peter,
    A double-beat metre,
And a load like the Biblical Flood.

❦

There was a young girl of Cape Cod
Who dreamt she'd been buggered by God.
    But it wasn't Jehovah
    That turned the girl over,
'Twas Roger the lodger, the sod!

❦

There was a young man in the choir
Whose penis rose higher and higher,
    Till it reached such a height
    It was quite out of sight—
But of course you know I'm a liar.

❦

There was a young woman in Dee
Who stayed with each man she did see.
    When it came to a test
    She wished to be best,
And practice makes perfect, you see.

There was an old man of Duluth
Whose cock was shot off in his youth.
    He fucked with his nose
    And with fingers and toes,
And he came through a hole in his tooth.

❦

A young man with passions quite gingery
Tore a hole in his sister's best lingerie.
    He slapped her behind
    And made up his mind
To add incest to insult and injury.

❦

There was a young lady named Gloria
Who was had by Sir Gerald Du Maurier,
    And then by six men,
    Sir Gerald again,
And the band at the Waldorf-Astoria.

❦

A newlywed couple from Goshen
Spent their honeymoon sailing the ocean.
    In twenty-eight days
    They got laid eighty ways—
Imagine such fucking devotion!

There was a young fellow named Grimes
Who fucked his girl seventeen times
    In the course of a week—
    And this isn't to speak
Of assorted venereal crimes.

❧

There was a young lady named Hatch
Who would always come through in a scratch.
    If a guy wouldn't neck her,
    She'd grab up his pecker
And shove the damn thing up her snatch.

❧

There was a young lady named Hilda
Who went for a walk with a builder.
    He knew that he could,
    And he should, and he would—
And he did—and he goddam near killed her!

❧

If you're speaking of actions immoral
Then how about giving the laurel
    To doughty Queen Esther,
    No three men could best her—
One fore, and one aft, and one oral.

There was a young fellow of Kent
Whose prick was so long that it bent,
    So to save himself trouble
    He put it in double,
And instead of coming he went.

❧

There was a young man of Kildare
Who was fucking a girl on the stair.
    The bannister broke,
    But he doubled his stroke
And finished her off in mid-air.

❧

There was a young girl from New York
Who plugged up her cunt with a cork.
    A woodpecker or two
    Made the grade, it is true,
But it totally baffled the stork.

Till along came a man who presented
A tool that was strangely indented.
    With a dizzying twirl
    He punctured that girl,
And thus was the cork-screw invented.

There was a young Scot in Madrid
Who got fifty-five fucks for a quid.
    When they said, " Are you faint? "
    He replied, " No, I ain't,
But I *don't* feel as good as I did. "

❦

A remarkable race are the Persians,
They have such peculiar diversions.
    They screw the whole day
    In the regular way,
And save up the nights for perversions.

❦

There was a young girl of Rangoon
Who was blocked by the Man in the Moon.
  " Well, it *has* been great fun, "
    She remarked when he'd done,
" But I'm sorry you came quite so soon. "

❦

There was a young lady named Ransom
Who was rogered three times in a hansom.
    When she cried out for more
    A voice from the floor
Said, " My name is Simpson, not Samson. "

" Last night, " said a lassie named Ruth,
" In a long-distance telephone booth,
I enjoyed the perfection
Of an ideal connection—
I was screwed, if you must know the truth."

There once was a handsome young seaman
Who with ladies was really a demon.
In peace or in war,
At sea or on shore,
He could certainly dish out the semen.

There was a young lady from Sydney
Who could take it right up to her kidney.
But a man from Quebec
Shoved it up to her neck.
He had a long one, now didn' he?

There was a young man of Tibet,
And this is the strangest one yet—
His prick was so long,
And so pointed and strong,
He could bugger six Greeks *en brochette.*

There was a young person of Kent
Who was famous wherever he went.
    All the way through a fuck
    He would quack like a duck,
And he crowed like a cock when he spent.

❧

A zoologist's daughter in Ewing
Gave birth to a bottle of bluing.
    Her father said, " Flo,
    What I want to know
Isn't *whether,* but *what* you've been screwing. "

❧

There was a young lady of Norway
Who hung by her heels in a doorway.
    She said to her beau,
    " Look at me, Joe,
I think I've discovered one more way. "

ORAL IRREGULARITY

❧

There once was a lady from Arden
Who sucked off a man in a garden.
    He said, " My dear Flo,
    Where does all that stuff go ? "
And she said, " (*swallow hard*)—I beg pardon ? "

❧

There was a young girl in Berlin
Who eked out a living through sin.
    She didn't mind fucking,
    But much preferred sucking,
And she'd wipe off the pricks on her chin.

❧

There was a young bride, a Canuck,
Told her husband, " Let's do more than suck.
    You say that I, maybe,
    Can have my first baby—
Let's give up this Frenching, and fuck ! "

King Louis gave a lesson in Class,
One time he was sexing a lass.
    When she used the word " Damn "
    He rebuked her : " Please ma'am,
Keep a more civil tongue in my ass. "

❦

There was an old man of Decatur,
Took out his red-hot pertater.
    He tried at her dent
    But when his thing bent,
He got down on his knees and he ate 'er.

❦

That naughty old Sappho of Greece
Said, " What I prefer to a piece
    Is to have my pudenda
    Rubbed hard by the enda
The little pink nose of my niece. "

❦

A canny Scotch lass named McFargle,
Without coaxing and such argy-bargle,
    Would suck a man's pud
    Just as hard as she could,
And she saved up the sperm for a gargle.

There was a young fellow named Meek
Who invented a lingual technique.
    It drove women frantic
    And made them romantic,
And wore all the hair off his cheek.

❧

There was a young man of Nantucket
Whose prick was so long he could suck it.
    He said with a grin,
    As he wiped off his chin,
" If my ear were a cunt I could fuck it. "

❧

There was a young fellow named Pell
Who didn't like cunt very well.
    He would finger and fuck one,
    But never would suck one—
He just couldn't get used to the smell.

❧

A young bride was once heard to say,
" Oh dear, I am wearing away!
    The insides of my thighs
    Look just like mince pies,
For my husband won't shave every day. "

A worried young man from Stamboul
Discovered red spots on his tool.
    Said the doctor, a cynic,
  " Get out of my clinic!
Just wipe off the lipstick, you fool. "

❧

A tidy young lady of Streator
Dearly loved to nibble a peter.
    She always would say,
  " I prefer it this way.
I think it is very much neater. "

❧

There was a young girl, very sweet,
Who thought sailors' meat quite a treat.
    When she sat on their lap
    She unbuttoned their flap,
And always had plenty to eat.

❧

There was a young fellow named Tucker
Who, instructing a novice cock-sucker,
    Said, " Don't bow out your lips
    Like an elephant's hips,
The boys like it best when they pucker. "

BUGGERY

❦

There was a young man of Arras
Who stretched himself out on the grass,
    And with no little trouble
    He bent himself double
And stuck his prick well up his ass.

❦

Coitus upon a cadaver
Is the ultimate way you can have 'er.
    Her inanimate state
    Means a man needn't wait,
And eliminates all the palaver.

❦

There was a young fellow named Dave
Who kept a dead whore in a cave.
    He said, " I admit
    I'm a bit of a shit,
But think of the money I save! "

An earnest young woman in Thrace
Said, "Darling, that's not the right place!"
So he gave her a thwack,
And did on her back
What he couldn't have done face to face.

There was a young lady who said,
As her bridegroom got into the bed,
"I'm tired of this stunt
That they do with one's cunt,
You can get up my bottom instead."

ABUSES OF THE CLERGY

There were three young ladies of Birmingham,
And this is the scandal concerning 'em.
They lifted the frock
And tickled the cock
Of the Bishop engaged in confirming 'em.

There was an old abbess quite shocked
To find nuns where the candles were locked.
    Said the abbess, " You nuns
    Should behave more like guns,
And never go off till you're cocked. "

There was a young monk from Siberia
Whose morals were very inferior.
    He did to a nun
    What he shouldn't have done,
And now she's a Mother Superior.

ZOOPHILY

There once was a fellow named Siegel
Who attempted to bugger a beagle,
    But the mettlesome bitch
    Turned and said with a twitch,
" It's fun, but you know it's illegal. "

There was a young girl from Decatur
Who was fucked by an old alligator.
    No one ever knew
    How she relished that screw,
For after he fucked her, he ate her.

❦

EXCREMENT

❦

There was a young man of Rangoon
Who farted and filled a balloon.
    The balloon went so high
    That it stuck in the sky,
And stank out the Man in the Moon.

❦

There was an old lady from Wheeling
Who had a peculiar feeling,
    She laid on her back
    And opened her crack
And pissed all over the ceiling.

GOURMANDS

There was a young fellow named Fritz
Who planted an acre of tits.
    They came up in the fall,
    Pink nipples and all,
And he chewed them all up into bits.

VIRGINITY

There was a young girl named Anheuser
Who said that no man could surprise her.
    But Pabst took a chance,
    Found Schlitz in her pants,
And now she is sadder Budweiser.

There was a young Miss from Cape Cod
Who at soldiers would not even nod.
    But she tripped in a ditch
    And some son-of-a-bitch
Of a corporal raped her, by God!

❦

A Salvation Lassie named Claire
Was having her first love affair.
    As she climbed into bed
    She reverently said,
"I wish to be opened with prayer."

❦

A girl named Alice, in Dallas,
Had never felt of a phallus.
    She remained virgo intacto,
    Because, ipso facto,
No phallus in Dallas fit Alice.

❦

There was a young girl of East Lynne
Whose mother, to save her from sin,
    Had filled up her crack
    To the brim with shellac,
But the boys picked it out with a pin.

There was a young fellow named Fyfe
Who married the pride of his life,
    But imagine his pain
    When he struggled in vain,
And just couldn't get into his wife.

❦

There was a young fellow named Gluck
Who found himself shit out of luck.
    Though he petted and wooed,
    When he tried to get screwed
He found virgins just don't give a fuck.

❦

There was a young girl named McKnight
Who got drunk with her boy-friend one night.
    She came to in bed
    With a split maidenhead—
That's the last time she ever was tight.

❦

There was a young girl from Sofia
Who succumbed to her lover's desire.
    She said, "It's a sin,
    But now that it's in,
Could you shove it a few inches higher?"

There was a young fellow named Sweeney
Whose girl was a terrible meanie.
    The hatch of her snatch
    Had a catch that would latch—
She could only be screwed by Houdini.

❦

A skinny old maid from Verdun
Wed a short-peckered son-of-a-gun.
    She said, " I don't care
    If there isn't much there.
God knows it is better than none. "

❦

There was a young lady called Wylde,
Who kept herself quite undefiled
    By thinking of Jesus,
    Contagious diseases,
And the bother of having a child.

MOTHERHOOD

❦

There once was a Vassar B.A.
Who pondered the problem all day
  Of what there would be
  If C-U-N-T
Were divided by C-O-C-K.

A young Ph.D. passing by,
She gave him the problem to try.
  He worked the division
  With perfect precision,
And the answer was B-A-B-Y.

❦

There was a young girl who begat
Three brats, by name Nat, Pat, and Tat.
  It was fun in the breeding
  But hell in the feeding,
When she found there was no tit for Tat.

There was a young pessimist, Grotton,
Who wished he had ne'er been begotten,
    Nor would he have been
    But the rubber was thin,
And right at the tip it was rotten.

❦

There was a young lady named Flo
Whose lover had pulled out too slow.
    So they tried it all night
    Till he got it just right...
Well, practice makes pregnant, you know.

❦

There was a young lady from Thrace
Whose corsets got too tight to lace.
    Her mother said, " Nelly,
    There's things in your belly
That never got in through your face. "

❦

There was a young lady named Myrtle
Whose womb was exceedingly fertile.
    Her pa got contortions
    At all her abortions,
And bought her a chastity girdle.

There was a young girl from Penzance
Who decided to take just one chance.
So she let herself go
In the lap of her beau,
And now all her sisters are aunts.

❧

There was a young lady named Sue
Who preferred a stiff drink to a screw.
But one leads to the other,
And now she's a mother—
Let this be a lesson to *you*.

❧

There was a young lady of Wantage
Of whom the Town Clerk took advantage.
Said the County Surveyor,
"Of course you must pay her;
You've altered the line of her frontage."

❧

There was a young lady of Maine
Who declared she'd a man on the brain.
But you knew from the view
Of the way her waist grew,
It was not on her brain that he'd lain.

PROSTITUTION

❦

There once was a floozie named Annie
Whose prices were cosy—but canny:
    A buck for a fuck,
    Fifty cents for a suck,
And a dime for a feel of her fanny.

❦

Said an elderly whore named Arlene,
"I prefer a young lad of eighteen.
    There's more cream in his larder,
    And his pecker gets harder,
And he fucks in a manner obscene."

❦

There was a young lady from Cue
Who filled her vagina with glue.
    She said with a grin,
  "If they pay to get in,
They'll pay to get out of it too."

There was a young girl named Dale
Who put up her ass for sale.
    For the sum of two bits
    You could tickle her tits,
But a buck would get you real tail.

❦

There was a young girl from Des Moines
Who had a large sack full of coins.
    The nickels and dimes
    She got from the times
That she cradled the boys in her loins.

❦

A notorious whore named Miss Hearst
In the weakness of men is well versed.
    Reads a sign o'er the head
    Of her well-rumpled bed:
"The customer always comes first."

❦

There was an old girl of Kilkenny
Whose usual charge was a penny.
    For the half of that sum
    You could finger her bum—
A source of amusement to many.

Said a madam named Mamie La Farge
To a sailor just off of a barge,
  "We have one girl that's dead,
  With a hole in her head—
Of course there's a slight extra charge."

❦

In the city of York there's a lass
Who will hitch up her dress when you pass.
  If you toss her two bits
  She will strip to the tits,
And let you explore her bare ass.

❦

A harlot of note named Le Dux
Would always charge seventy bucks.
  But for that she would suck you,
  And wink-off and fuck you—
The whole thing was simply de luxe!

❦

There was a young whore from Madrid
Who anyone could fuck for a quid.
  But a bastard Italian
  With balls like a stallion
Said he'd do it for nothing—and did.

Unique is a strumpet of Mazur
In the way that her clientèle pays her:
    A machine that she uses
    Clamps on to her whoosis,
And clocks everybody that lays her.

❦

There was an old whore named McGee
Who was just the right sort for a spree.
    She said, "For a fuck
    I charge half a buck,
And I throw in the ass-hole for free."

❦

Said a dainty young whore named Miss Meggs,
"The men like to spread my two legs,
    Then slip in between,
    If you know what I mean,
And leave me the white of their eggs."

❦

Said Clark Gable, picking his nose,
"I get more than the public suppose.
    Take the Hollywood way,
    It's the women who pay,
And the men simply take off their clothes."

There was a young lady in Reno
Who lost all her dough playing keeno.
    But she lay on her back
    And opened her crack,
And now she owns the casino.

❦

DuPont, I. G., Monsanto, and Shell
Built a world-circling pussy cartel,
    And by planned obsolescence
    So controlled detumescence
A poor man could not get a smell.

❦

There was a hot girl from the Saar
Who fucked all, both from near and from far.
    When asked to explain,
    She replied with disdain,
" I'm trying to buy me a car. "

❦

There was a young girl from St. Cyr
Whose reflex reactions were queer.
    Her escort said, " Mable,
    Get up off the table;
That money's to pay for the beer. "

A licentious old justice of Salem
Used to catch all the harlots and jail 'em.
    But instead of a fine
    He would stand them in line,
With his common-law tool to impale 'em.

❦

Ethnologists up with the Sioux
Wired home for two punts, one canoe.
    The answer next day
    Said, "Girls on the way,
But what the hell's a 'panoe'?"

❦

There was an old Count of Swoboda
Who would not pay a whore what he owed her.
    So with great *savoir-faire*
    She stood on a chair,
And pissed in his whiskey-and-soda.

❦

There was an old man of Tagore
Who tried out his cook as a whore
    He used Bridget's twidget
    To fidget his digit,
And now she won't cook any more.

A young girl who was no good at tennis,
But at swimming was really a menace,
    Took pains to explain,
  " It depends how you train :
I was a street-walker in Venice. "

❦

There once was a harlot at Yale
With her price-list tattooed on her tail,
    And on her behind,
    For the sake of the blind,
She had it embroidered in Braille.

❦

The chief charm of a whore in Shalott
Was the absence of hair on her twat.
    She kept it smooth-looking
    Not by shaving or plucking,
But by all of the fucking she got.

DISEASES

❦

A sultan named Abou ben Adhem
Thus cautioned a travelling madam,
  " I suffer from crabs
    As do most us A-rabs, "
" It's alright, " said the madam, " I've had 'em. "

❦

There was a young woman of Chester
Who said to the man who undressed her,
  " I think you will find
    That it's better behind—
The front is beginning to fester. "

❦

There was a young rounder named Fisk
Whose method of screwing was brisk.
    And his reason was : " If
    The damned bitch has the syph,
This way I'm reducing the risk. "

There was a young lady named Hitchin
Who was scratching her crotch in the kitchen.
    Her mother said, "Rose,
    It's the crabs, I suppose."
She said, "Yes, and the buggers are itchin'."

❦

There was a young maid of Klepper
Went out one night with a stepper,
    And now in dismay
    She murmurs each day,
"His pee-pee was made of red-pepper!"

❦

A charming young lady named Randall
Has a clap that the doctors can't handle.
    So this lovely, lorn floozie,
    With her poor, damaged coosie,
Must take her delight with a candle.

❦

There was a young lady at sea
Who said, "God, how it hurts me to pee."
  "I see," said the mate,
  "That accounts for the state
Of the captain, the purser, and me."

A fellow who slept with a whore
Used a safe, but his pecker got sore.
    Said he with chagrin,
  " Selling these is a sin. "
Said the druggist, " *Caveat emptor.* "

There once was a writer named Twain
Who had a peculiar stain
    Surrounding the head
    Of his prick : it was red,
And was said to wash off in the rain.

LOSSES

There was a young sailor named Bates
Who did the fandango on skates.
    He fell on his cutlass
    Which rendered him nutless
And practically useless on dates.

There was a young fellow from Boston
Who rode around in an Austin.
    There was room for his ass
    And a gallon of gas,
But his balls hung outside, and he lost 'em.

❦

There was a young man of Canute
Who was troubled by warts on his root.
    He put acid on these,
    And now, when he pees,
He can finger his root like a flute.

❦

There was a young girl in a cast
Who had an unsavory past,
    For the neighborhood pastor
    Tried fucking through plaster,
And his very first fuck was his last.

❦

There was a young lady of Clewer
Who was riding a bike, and it threw her.
    A man saw her there
    With her legs in the air,
And seized the occasion to screw her.

There was a young lady named Duff
With a lovely, luxuriant muff.
    In his haste to get in her
    One eager beginner
Lost both of his balls in the rough.

❦

And then there's a story that's fraught
With disaster—of balls that got caught,
    When a chap took a crap
    In the woods, and a trap
Underneath... Oh, I can't bear the thought!

❦

There was a young man from Glenchasm
Who had a tremendous orgasm.
    In the midst of his thralls
    He burst both his balls
And covered an acre with plasm.

❦

There was a young man in Havana,
Fucked a girl on a player piano.
    At the height of their fever
    Her ass hit the lever—
Yes! He has no banana!

There was a young man with a hernia
Who said to his surgeon, "Gol-dernya,
When carving my middle
Be sure you don't fiddle
With matters that do not concernya."

❧

There was a young couple named Kelly
Who had to live belly to belly,
Because once, in their haste,
They used library paste
Instead of petroleum jelly.

❧

There was a young man of Khartoum
Who lured a poor girl to her doom.
He not only fucked her,
But buggered and sucked her—
And left her to pay for the room.

❧

Did you hear about young Henry Lockett?
He was blown down the street by a rocket.
The force of the blast
Blew his balls up his ass,
And his pecker was found in his pocket.

There was a young man of Madras
Who was fucking a girl in the grass,
    But the tropical sun
    Spoiled half of his fun
By singeing the hair off his ass.

❦

There was a young man of Missouri
Who fucked with a terrible fury,
    Till hauled into court
    For his besti-al sport,
And condemned by a poorly-hung jury.

❦

All winter the eunuch from Munich
Went walking in naught but a tunic.
    Folks said, " You've a cough;
    You'll freeze your balls off! "
Said he, " That's why I'm a eunuch. "

❦

There was a young lady named Nance
Whose lover had St. Vitus dance.
    When she dove for his prick,
    He wriggled so quick,
She bit a piece out of his pants.

There was an old man from New York
Whose tool was as dry as a cork.
    While attempting to screw
    He split it in two,
And now his tool is a fork.

❧

One evening a workman named Rawls
Fell asleep in his old overalls.
    And when he woke up he
    Discovered a puppy
Had bitten off both of his balls.

❧

A horny young fellow named Redge
Was jerking off under a hedge.
    The gardener drew near
    With a huge pruning shear,
And trimmed off the edge of his wedge.

❧

When the White Man attempted to rule
The Indians made him a fool.
    They cut off his nuts
    To hang in their huts,
And stuffed up his mouth with his tool.

There was a young singer named Springer,
Got his testicles caught in the wringer.
    He hollered with pain
    As they rolled down the drain,
(*falsetto*) : " There goes my career as a singer! "

❦

There was an old rake from Stamboul
Felt his ardor grow suddenly cool.
    No lack of affection
    Reduced his erection—
But his zipper got caught in his tool.

❦

There was a young girl of high station
Who ruined her fine reputation
    When she said she'd the pox
    From sucking on cocks—
She should really have called it " fellation. "

❦

I'd rather have fingers than toes,
I'd rather have ears than a nose,
    And a happy erection
    Brought just to perfection
Makes me terribly sad when it goes.

There was a young lady of Wheeling
Who professed to lack sexual feeling.
    But a cynic named Boris
    Just touched her clitoris,
And she had to be scraped off the ceiling.

SEX SUBSTITUTES

A man in the battle of Aix
Had one nut and his cock shot away,
    But found out in this pickle
    His nose could still tickle,
Though he might get the snuffles some day.

Nymphomaniacal Alice
Used a dynamite stick for a phallus.
    They found her vagina
    In North Carolina,
And her ass-hole in Buckingham Palace.

A lesbian lassie named Anny
Desired to appear much more manny.
    So she whittled a pud
    Of mahogany wood,
And let it protrude from her cranny.

❧

A nudist resort at Benares
Took a midget in all unawares.
    But he made members weep
    For he just couldn't keep
His nose out of private affairs.

❧

A squeamish young fellow named Brand
Thought caressing his penis was grand,
    But he viewed with distaste
    The gelatinous paste
That it left in the palm of his hand.

❧

There was a young woman of Croft
Who played with herself in a loft,
    Having reasoned that candles
    Could never cause scandals,
Besides which they did not go soft.

There was a young man from Darjeeling
Whose dong reached up to the ceiling.
    In the electric light socket
    He'd put it and rock it—
Oh God! What a wonderful feeling!

❧

A certain young fellow named Dick
Liked to feel a girl's hand on his prick.
    He taught them to fool
    With his rigid old tool
Till the cream shot out, white and thick.

❧

An agreeable girl named Miss Doves
Likes to jack off the young men she loves.
    She will use her bare fist
    If the fellows insist
But she really prefers to wear gloves.

❧

A fair-haired young damsel named Grace
Thought it very, very foolish to place
    Her hand on your cock
    When it turned hard as rock,
For fear it would explode in her face.

There was a young parson of Harwich,
Tried to grind his betrothed in a carriage.
    She said, "No, you young goose,
    Just try self-abuse.
And the other we'll try after marriage."

❦

A neurotic young man of Kildare
Drilled a hole in the seat of a chair.
    He fucked it all night,
    Then died of the fright
That maybe he wasn't "all there."

❦

She made a thing of soft leather,
And topped off the end with a feather.
    When she poked it inside her
    She took off like a glider,
And gave up her lover forever.

❦

A thrifty old man named McEwen
Inquired, "Why be bothered with screwing?
    It's safer and cleaner
    To finger your wiener,
And besides you can see what you're doing."

A lusty young woodsman of Maine
For years with no woman had lain,
    But he found sublimation
    At a high elevation
In the crotch of a pine—God, the pain!

❧

There was a young lady named Mandel
Who caused quite a neighborhood scandal
    By coming out bare
    On the main village square
And frigging herself with a candle.

❧

There was a young girl of Mobile
Whose hymen was made of chilled steel.
    To give her a thrill
    Took a rotary drill
Or a Number 9 emery wheel.

❧

There was a young man from Montrose
Who could diddle himself with his toes.
    He did it so neat
    He fell in love with his feet,
And christened them Myrtle and Rose.

There was a young lady from Munich
Who was had in a park by a eunuch.
    In a moment of passion
    He shot her a ration
From a squirt-gun concealed 'neath his tunic.

❦

There was a young man in Norway,
Tried to jerk himself off in a sleigh,
    But the air was so frigid
    It froze his balls rigid,
And all he could come was frappé.

❦

A bobby of Nottingham Junction
Whose organ had long ceased to function
    Deceived his good wife
    For the rest of her life
With the aid of his constable's truncheon.

❦

There was a young fellow named Perkin
Who always was jerkin' his gherkin.
    His wife said, "Now, Perkin,
    Stop jerkin' your gherkin;
You're shirkin' your ferkin'—you bastard!"

There was a young man named Pete
Who was a bit indiscreet.
    He pulled on his dong
    Till it grew very long
And actually dragged in the street.

❦

There was a young man from Racine
Who invented a fucking machine.
    Concave or convex
    It would fit either sex,
With attachments for those in between.

❦

There was a young girl named Miss Randall
Who thought it beneath her to handle
    A young fellow's pole,
    So instead, her hot hole
She contented by means of a candle.

❦

There was a young lady named Rose
Who'd occasionally straddle a hose,
    And parade about, squirting
    And spouting and spurting,
Pretending she pissed like her beaux.

There was a young lady named Rose,
With erogenous zones in her toes.
    She remained onanistic
    Till a foot-fetichistic
Young man became one of her beaux.

❦

There once was a eunuch of Roylem,
Took two eggs to the cook and said, "Boil 'em.
    I'll sling 'em beneath
    My inadequate sheath,
And slip into the harem and foil 'em."

❦

There's a pretty young lady named Sark,
Afraid to get laid in the dark,
    But she's often manhandled
    By the light of a candle
In the bushes of Gramercy Park.

❦

A milkmaid there was, with a stutter,
Who was lonely and wanted a futter.
    She had nowhere to turn,
    So she diddled a churn,
And managed to come with the butter.

There was a young fellow named Veach
Who fell fast asleep on the beach.
    His dreams of nude women
    Had his proud organ brimming
And squirting on all within reach.

❧

There was a young fellow from Yale
Whose face was exceedingly pale.
    He spent his vacation
    In self-masturbation
Because of the high price of tail.

❧

There was a young man from Winsocket
Who put a girl's hand in his pocket.
    Her delicate touch
    Thrilled his pecker so much,
It shot off in the air like a rocket.

ASSORTED ECCENTRICITIES

Floating idly one day through the air
A circus performer named Blair
    Tied a sizeable rock
    To the end of his cock
And shattered a balcony chair.

There was a young man of Australia
Who painted his ass like a dahlia.
    The drawing was fine,
    The color divine,
The scent—ah, that was a failure.

The Reverend Henry Ward Beecher
Called a girl a most elegant creature.
    So she laid on her back
    And, exposing her crack,
Said, "Fuck *that*, you old Sunday School Teacher!"

There was a young man of Belgravia
Who cared neither for God nor his Saviour.
    He walked down the Strand
    With his prick in his hand
And was jailed for indecent behavior.

❧

A vigorous fellow named Bert
Was attracted by every new skirt.
    Oh, it wasn't their minds
    But their rounded behinds
That excited this loveable flirt.

❧

A lazy, fat fellow named Betts
Upon his fat ass mostly sets.
    Along comes a gal
    And says, "*I*'ll fuck you, pal."
Says he, "If you'll do the work, let's."

❧

There was a young fellow named Bliss
Whose sex life was strangely amiss,
    For even with Venus
    His recalcitrant penis
Would never do better than t
h
i
s
.

There once was an actress of Bonely,
And the men never let her be lonely.
    So she hung out in front
    Of her popular cunt
A sign reading : " Standing Room Only. "

❦

There was a gay Countess of Bray,
And you may think it odd when I say,
    That in spite of high station,
    Rank and education,
She always spelt Cunt with a K.

❦

There was a young lady named Bruce
Who captured her man by a ruse :
    She filled up her fuselage
    With a good grade of mucilage,
And he never could pry himself loose.

❦

There was a young fellow named Chick
Who fancied himself rather slick.
    He went to a ball
    Dressed in nothing at all
But a big velvet bow round his prick.

There was a young lady from China
Who mistook for her mouth her vagina.
    Her clitoris huge
    She covered with rouge
And lipsticked her labia minor.

❦

An ignorant maiden named Crewe-Pitt
Did something amazingly stupid :
    When her lover had spent
    She douched with cement,
And gave birth to a statue of Cupid.

❦

There was a young man of Datchet
Who cut off his prick with a hatchet.
    Then very politely
    He sent it to Whitely,
And ordered a cunt that would match it.

❦

There was a young fellow named Dick
Who perfected a wonderful trick :
    With a safe for protection
    He'd get an erection,
And then balance himself on his prick.

A psychoneurotic fanatic
Said, " I take little girls to the attic,
Then whistle a tune
'Bout the cow and the moon—
When the cow jumps, I come. It's dramatic. "

❦

There was an old fellow named Fletcher,
A lewd and perverted old lecher.
In a spirit of meanness
He cut off his penis,
And now he regrets it, I betcha.

❦

Said Einstein, " I have an equation
Which science might call Rabelaisian.
Let P be virginity
Approaching infinity,
And U be a constant, persuasion.

" Now if P over U be inverted
And the square root of U be inserted
X times over P,
The result, Q.E.D.
Is a relative, " Einstein asserted.

There was a young girlie named Hannah
Who loved madly her lover's banana.
    She loved pubic hair
    And balls that were bare,
And she jacked him off in her bandanna.

❧

A sensitive fellow named Harry
Thought sex too revolting to marry.
    So he went out in curls
    And frowned on the girls,
And he got to be known as a fairy.

❧

There was an announcer named Herschel
Whose habits became controversial,
    Because when out wooing
    Whatever he was doing
At ten he'd insert his commercial.

❧

There was a young lady named Hicks
Who delighted to play with men's pricks,
    Which she would embellish
    With evident relish,
And make them stand up and do tricks.

There was a young girl from Hong Kong
Whose cervical cap was a gong.
    She said with a yell,
    As a shot rang the bell,
" I'll give you a ding for a dong. "

❦

There was a young man in Hong Kong
Who grew seven fathoms of prong.
    It looked, when erect,
    About as you'd expect—
When coiled it did not seem so long.

❦

That horny old rascal, Manet,
While buggering a boy on the Quay,
    Was attacked by a crick
    In the tip of his prick—
" *Merde!* " he cried, " Quick! Baume Bengué! "

❦

Regardez-vous Toulouse-Lautrec,
Though at first glance an ambulant wreck,
    He could fuck once a week
    A la manière antique,
And once in a while *à la Grecque.*

Van Gogh found a whore who would lay,
And accept a small painting as pay.
  " *Vive l'Art!* " cried Van Gogh,
  " But it's too fucking slow—
I wish I could paint ten a day! "

❦

For sculpture that's really first class
You need form, composition, and mass.
  To do a good Venus
  Just leave off the penis,
And concentrate all on the ass.

❦

A young man who lived in Khartoum
Was exceedingly fond of the womb.
  He thought nothing finer
  Than the human vagina,
So he kept three or four in his room.

❦

The last time I dined with the King
He did quite a curious thing:
  He sat on a stool
  And took out his tool,
And said, " If I play, will you sing? "

There was a young lady named Knox
Who kept a pet snake in her box.
    It was trained not to hiss
    When she sat down to piss,
But would nibble the noggins off cocks.

There was a young laundress of Lamas
Who invented high amorous dramas
    For the spots she espied
    Dried and hardened inside
The pants of the parson's pajamas.

There once was a spinsterish lass
Who constructed her panties of brass.
    When asked, "Do they chafe?"
    She said, "Yes, but I'm safe
Against pinches, and pins in the ass."

There once was a girl named Louise
Whose cunt-hair hung down to her knees.
    The crabs in her twat
    Tied the hair in a knot,
And constructed a flying trapeze.

The team of Tom and Louise
Do an act in the nude on their knees.
    They crawl down the aisle
    While fucking dog-style,
And the orchestra plays Kilmer's "Trees."

❦

Have you heard about Magda Lupescu,
Who came to Rumania's rescue?
    It's a wonderful thing
    To be under a king—
Is democracy better, I esk you?

❦

A golfer named Sandy MacFarr
Went to bed with a Hollywood star
    When he first saw her gash he
    Cried, "Quick, goot muh mashie!
Uh thunk uh c'n muk it in par."

❦

A bus-man named Abner McFuss
Liked to suck off small boys on his bus,
    Then go out and sniff turds
    And the assholes of birds—
He sure was a funny old cuss.

There was a young man from Mobile
Who wondered just how it would feel
To carry a gong
Hanging down from his dong,
And occasionally let the thing peal.

So he rigged up a clever device,
And tried the thing out once or twice,
But it wasn't the gong
But rather his prong
That peeled, and it didn't feel nice!

❦

There was a young girl of Moline
Whose fucking was sweet and obscene.
She would work on a prick
With every known trick,
And finish by winking it clean.

❦

There was a young farmer of Nant
Whose conduct was gay and gallant,
For he fucked all his dozens
Of nieces and cousins,
In addition, of course, to his aunt.

There was a young man from Naragansett
Who colored his prick to enhance it.
    But the girls were afraid
    That ere they got laid
'Twould lose all its color in transit.

❧

There was a young fellow named Price
Who dabbled in all sorts of vice.
    He had virgins and boys
    And mechanical toys,
And on Mondays... he meddled with mice!

❧

A detective named Ellery Queen
Has olfactory powers so keen,
    He can tell in a flash
    By the scent of a gash
Who its previous tenant has been.

❧

There was a young man from Racine
Who was weaned at the age of sixteen.
    He said, "I'll admit
    There's no milk in the tit,
But think of the fun it has been."

The cock of a fellow named Randall
Shot sparks like a big Roman candle.
He was much in demand,
For the colors were grand,
But the girls found him too hot to handle.

❦

A widow who lived in Rangoon
Hung a black-ribboned wreath on her womb,
" To remind me, " she said,
" Of my husband who's dead,
And of what put him into his tomb. "

❦

There was a young man of St. James
Who indulged in the jolliest games :
He lighted the rim
Of his grandmother's quim,
And laughed as she pissed through the flames.

❦

There was a young man from St. Paul's
Who read *Harper's Bazaar* and *McCall's*
Till he grew such a passion
For feminine fashion
That he knitted a snood for his balls.

There were three young girls in St. Thomas,
Arrived at a dance in pajamas.
    They got screwed by the drummer,
    And this went on all summer—
I'm surprised that by now they ain't mamas.

❧

There was a young lady named Smith
Whose virtue was largely a myth.
    She said, " Try as I can
    I can't find a man
Who it's fun to be virtuous with. "

❧

There once was a Monarch of Spain
Who was terribly haughty and vain.
    When women were nigh
    He'd unbutton his fly,
And screw them with signs of disdain.

❧

When the judge, with his wife having sport,
Proved suddenly two inches short,
    The good woman declined,
    And the judge had her fined
By proving contempt of the court.

" I'll admit, " said a lady named Starr,
" That a phallus is like a cigar;
  But to most common people
  A phallic church-steeple
Is stretching the matter too far. "

❦

There was a composer so swell
Who thought screwing to music was hell.
  Everything went fine
  Till he got out of time—
" Say, this isn't Bach, it's Ravel! "

❦

The mathematician Von Blecks
Devised an equation for sex,
  Having proved a good fuck
  Isn't patience or luck,
But a function of *y* over *x*.

❦

There was a young female named Ware
Who cut off her pubical hair.
  Then to save the men trouble
  She razored the stubble,
But none of them really did care.

WEAK SISTERS

There was a young woman from Aenos
Who came to our party as Venus.
We told her how rude
'Twas to come there quite nude,
And we brought her a leaf from the green-h'us.

A girl attending Bryn Mawr
Committed a dreadful faux pas.
She loosened a stay
In her decolleté,
Exposing her je-ne-sais-quoi.

A lady athletic and handsome
Got wedged in her sleeping room transom.
When she offered much gold
For release, she was told
That the view was worth more than the ransom.

There was a young girl of Oak Knoll
Who thought it exceedingly droll,
At a masquerade ball
Dressed in nothing at all
To back in as a Parker House roll.

There was a young maid from Madras
Who had a magnificent ass;
Not rounded and pink,
As you probably think—
It was grey, had long ears, and ate grass.

There was an old sculptor named Phidias
Whose knowledge of Art was invidious.
He carved Aphrodite
Without any nightie—
Which startled the purely fastidious.

There's a man in the Bible portrayed
As one deeply engrossed in his trade.
He became quite elated
Over things he created,
Especially the women he made.

A king sadly said to his queen,
" In parts you have grown far from lean. "
  " I don't give a damn,
    You've always liked ham, "
She replied, and he gasped, " How obscene! "

❧

I sat next to the Duchess at tea.
It was just as I feared it would be :
    Her rumblings abdominal
    Were simply phenomenal,
And everyone thought it was me!

❧

There was a young lady of Trent
Who said that she knew what it meant
    When he asked her to dine,
    Private room, lots of wine,
She knew, oh she knew!—but she went!

❧

There was a young lady from Wheeling
Who was out in the garden a-kneeling,
    When by some strange chance
    She got ants in her pants,
And invented Virginia reeling.

CHAMBER OF HORRORS

There was a young fellow named Louvies
Who tickled his girl in the boovies,
    And as she contorted,
    He looked down and snorted,
" My prick wants to get in your movies! "

There once was a gangster named Brown,
The wiliest bastard in town.
    He was caught by the G-men
    Shooting his semen
Where the cops would all slip and fall down.

There was a young fellow from Eno
Who said to his girl, " Now, old Beano,
    Lift your skirt up in front,
    And enlarge your old cunt,
For the size of this organ is keen-o. "

DIRTIER LITTLE LIMERICKS

There was a young lady of Exeter,
So pretty, that men craned their necks at her.
  One went so far
  As to wave from his car
The distinguishing mark of his sex at her.

There was a young fellow named Scott
Who took a girl out on his yacht–
  But too lazy to rape her
  He made darts of brown paper,
Which he languidly tossed at her twat.

"I insist." "It's no good." "But you must."
"Think of me." "Think of masculine lust."
  "What a bore." "Why, you whore!
  You promised before."
"And the mink! Is that got through trust?"

An ancient but jolly old bloke
Once picked up a girl for a poke;
   First took down her pants,
   Fucked her into a trance,
Then shit in her shoe for a joke.

There was a young lady named Dowd
Whom a young fellow groped in the crowd.
   But the thing that most vexed her
   Was that when he stood next her
He said, "How's your cunt?" right out loud.

There was a young student of Trinity
Who shattered his sister's virginity.
   He buggered his brother,
   Had twins by his mother,
And took double honours in Divinity.

The gay young Duke of Buckingham
Stood on the bridge at Rockingham
   Watching the stunts
   Of the cunts and the punts
And the tricks of the pricks that were fucking 'em.

Said Oscar McDingle O'Figgle,
With an almost hysterical giggle,
"Last night I was sick
With delight when my prick
Felt dear Alfred's delicious ass wriggle!"

A vice both obscure and unsavory
Kept the Bishop of Chester in slavery:
Midst terrible howls
He deflowered young owls
In his crypt fitted out as an aviary.

A hermit who had an oasis
Thought it the best of all places:
He could pray and be calm
'Neath a pleasant date-palm,
While the lice on his ballocks ran races.

"Fuck me quick, fuck me deep, fuck me oft
In the bog, in the bath, in the loft,
Up my ass, up my quim,
Knees, armpits, lip rim
With your prick, but *please*, nothing soft."

A preposterous King of Siam
Said, "For women I don't care a damn.
    But a fat-bottomed boy
    Is my pride and my joy–
They call me a bugger: I am!"

❧

There are three ladies of Huxham,
And whenever we meets 'em we fucks 'em.
    When that game grows stale
    We sits on a rail,
Pulls out our pricks, and they sucks 'em.

❧

Then up spake the Bey of Algiers,
"I've been knocking around for long years,
    And my language is blunt:
    A cunt IS a cunt
And fucking IS fucking"–(loud cheers).

Hearing this, mewed the young King of Spain,
"To fuck and to bugger is shame.
    But it's not *infra dig.*
    To occasionally frig–
So I do it again and again."

When Titian was mixing rose madder,
His model was poised on a ladder.
  "Your position," said Titian,
  "Inspires coition."
So he nipped up the ladder and 'ad 'er.

An organist playing in York
Had a prick that could hold a small fork.
  And between obligatos
  He'd much at tomatoes,
And keep up his strength while at work.

It always delights me at Hanks
To walk up the old river banks.
  One time in the grass
  I stepped on an ass,
And heard a young girl murmur, "Thanks!"

"Far dearer to me than my treasure,"
The heiress declared, "is my leisure.
  For then I can screw
  The whole Harvard crew–
They're slow, but that lengthens the pleasure."

There was a young man from the Coast
Who had an affair with a ghost.
   At the height of the orgasm
   Said the pallid phantasm,
"I think I can feel it—almost!"

❧

There was a young lady from Kew
Who filled her vagina with glue.
   She said with a grin,
   "If they pay to get in,
They'll pay to get out of it too."

❧

Here's to it, and through it, and to it again,
To suck it, and screw it, and screw it again!
   So in with it, out with it,
   Lord work his will with it!
Never a day we don't do it again!

❧

There was a debauched little wench
Whom nothing could ever make blench.
   She admitted men's poles
   At all possible holes,
And she'd bugger, fuck, jerk off, and french.

There was a young man of Coblenz
Whose ballocks were simply immense:
  It took forty-four draymen,
  A priest and three laymen
To carry them thither and thence.

There was a young maid named Clottery
Who was having a fuck on a rockery.
  She said, "Listen chum,
  You've come on my bum!
This isn't a fuck, it's a mockery."

A sweet young strip-dancer named Jane
Wore five inches of thin cellophane.
  When asked why she wore it
  She said, "I abhor it,
But my cunt juice would spatter like rain."

An agreeable girl named Miss Doves
Likes to jack off the young men she loves.
  She will use her bare fist
  If the fellows insist
But she really prefers to wear gloves.

The Rajah of Afghanistan
Imported a Birmingham can,
   Which he set as a throne
   On a great Buddha stone–
But he crapped out-of-doors like a man.

A scandal involving an oyster
Sent the Countess of Clewes to a cloister,
   She preferred it in bed
   To the Count, so she said,
Being longer, and stronger, and moister.

A lady on climbing Mount Shasta
Complained as the mountain grew vaster,
   That it wasn't the climb
   Nor the dirt and the grime,
But the ice on her ass that harassed her.

When a woman in strapless attire
Found her breasts working higher and higher,
   A guest, with great feeling,
   Exclaimed, "How appealing!
Do you mind if I piss in the fire?"

There was a young Angel called Cary
Who kissed, stroked and fucked Virgin Mary.
   And Christ was so bored
   At seeing Mom whored
That he set Himself up as a fairy.

There was a young girl of Devon
Who was raped in the garden by seven
   High Anglican Priests–
   The lascivious beasts–
Of such is the kingdom of Heaven.

There was a young man of Bengal
Who went to a fancy dress ball.
   He was draped like a tree
   Having failed to foresee
Being pissed on by dogs, cats, and all.

A maiden who lived in Virginny
Had a cunt that could bark, neigh and whinny.
   The hunting set chased her,
   Fucked, buggered, then dropped her
For the pitch of her organ went tinny.

" 'Tis my custom," said dear Lady Norris,
"To beg lifts from the drivers of lorries.
   When they get out to piss
   I see things that I miss
At the wheel of my two-seater Morris."

A mediaeval recluse named Sissions
Was alarmed by his nightly emissions.
   His cell-mate, a sod,
   Said, "Leave it to God."
And taught him some nifty positions.

In the city of Paris are wives
Who, when not scratching their hives,
   Are waiting for tourists
   Who might act as purists
And give them the ride of their lives.

There was a young artist named Frentzel
Whose tool was as sharp as a pencil.
   He pricked through an actress,
   The sheet and the mattress,
And busted the bedroom utensil.

All the lady-apes ran from King Kong
For his dong was unspeakably long.
  But a friendly giraffe
  Quaffed his yard and a half,
And ecstatically burst into song.

The prior of Dunstan St. Just,
Consumed with erotical lust,
  Raped the bishop's prize fowls,
  Buggered four startled owls
And a little green lizard, that bust.

"In my salad days," said Lady Bierley,
"I took my cocks fairly and squarely.
  But now when they come
  They go right up my bum–
And that only happens but rarely."

The Marquesa de Excusador
Used to pee on the drawing-room floor,
  For the can was so cold
  And when one grows old
To be much alone is a bore.

"It's been a very full day,"
Yawned Lady Mary McDougle McKay.
"Three cherry tarts,
At least twenty farts,
Two shits and a bloody fine lay."

An elderly pervert in Nice
Who was long past wanting a piece
Would jack-off his hogs,
His cows and his dogs,
Till his parrot called in the police.

"Great God!" wailed Peter McGuff,
What the devil is all of this stuff!
She twiddles my prick,
Gets it stiff as a stick,
And denies me the use of her muff."

There was a young parson named Binns
Who talked about women and things.
But his secret desire
Was a boy in the choir
With a bottom like jelly on springs.

There was a young Scot of Delray
Who buggered his father one day,
Saying, "I like it rather
To stuff it up Father;
He's clean–and there's nothing to pay."

There was an old man of Dundee,
Who came home as drunk as could be.
He wound up the clock
With the end of his cock,
And buggared his wife with the key.

There was an old critic named West
Whose penis came up to his chest.
He said, "I declare,
I have no pubic hair."
So he covered his nuts with his vest.

The nephew of one of the czars
Used to suck off Rasputin at Yars,
'Til the peasants revolted,
The royal family bolted–
Now they're under the sickle and stars.

There was a young lady named Alice
Who was having a piss in a chalice.
"What a stunt," said a monk,
"To twiddle your cunt,
Not through need but through Protestant malice."

❧

There was a young student named Howells
Shot his sperm o'er a young coed's bowels.
He said, "I regret
That I've made you so wet–
And I fear I am quite out of towels."

❧

There was an old man who could piss
Through a ring–and what's more, never miss.
Marksmen queued up to cheer,
Bought him beer after beer,
And swore oaths on his urinal hiss.

❧

There was a young man of high station
Who was found by a pious relation
Making love in a ditch
To–I won't say a bitch–
But a woman of *no* reputation.

A broken-down harlot named Tupps
Was heard to confess in her cups:
"The height of my folly
Was fucking a collie–
But I got a nice price for the pups."

A passionate red-headed girl,
When you kissed her, her senses would whirl,
And her twat would get wet
And would wiggle and fret,
And her cunt-lips would curl and unfurl.

There was a young man from Lynn
Whose cock was the size of a pin.
Said his girl with a laugh
As she fondled his staff,
"This won't be much of a sin."

To his bride a young bridegroom said, "Pish!
Your cunt is as big as a dish!"
She replied, "Why, you fool,
With your limp little tool
It's like driving a nail with a fish!"

There was a young fellow named Brewster
Who said to his wife as he goosed her,
  "It used to be grand
  But just look at my hand!
You ain't wiping as clean as you used to."

There was a young girl named McCall
Whose cunt was exceedingly small,
  But the size of her anus
  Was something quite heinous–
It could hold seven pricks and one ball.

A cretin who lived in an attic
Was fallaciously rated as static;
  But how little they knew–
  His knob was not blue–
But hoary and necrophilatic.

There was a young girl of Dundee
Who was raped by an ape in a tree.
  The result was most horrid–
  All ass and no forehead,
Three balls and a purple goatee.

Thus spake I AM THAT I AM:
"For the Virgin I don't give a damn,
What pleases me most
Is to bugger the Ghost,
And then be sucked off by the Lamb."

When a lecherous curate at Leeds
Was discovered, one day, in the weeds
Astride a young nun,
He said, "Christ, this is fun!
Far better than telling one's beads!"

There was a young lady of Crewe
Whose cherry a chap had got through–
Which she told to her mother
Who fixed her another
Out of rubber and red ink and glue.

There was a young dancer, Priscilla,
Who flavored her cunt with vanilla.
The taste was so fine,
Men and beasts stood in line,
Including a stud armadilla.

The priest, a cocksucker named Sheen,
Is delighted his sins are not seen.
"Though God sees through walls,"
Says Monsignor, "–Oh, balls!
This God stuff is simply a screen."

There was a young girl in Alsace
Who was having her first piece of ass.
"Oh, darling you'll kill me!
Oh, dearest, you thrill me
Like Father John's thumb after mass!"

A modern young lady named Hall
Went out to a birth-controll ball.
She was loaded with pessaries
And other accessories,
But no one approached her at all.

A handsome young monk in a wood
Told a girl she should cling to the good.
She obeyed him, and gladly;
He repulsed her, but sadly:
"My dear, you have misunderstood."

There was a young man of St. Johns
Who wanted to bugger the swans.
"Oh no," said the porter,
"You bugger my daughter,
Them swans is reserved for the Dons."

There was a young man from Axminster
Whose designs were quite base and quite sinister.
His lifelong ambition
Was anal coition
With the wife of the French foreign minister.

A team playing baseball in Dallas
Called the umpire a shit out of malice.
While this worthy had fits,
The team made eight hits
And a girl in the bleachers named Alice.

"For the tenth time, dull Daphnis," said Chloe,
"You have told me my bosom is snowy;
You have made much fine verse on
Each part of my person,
Now *do* something– there's a good boy!"

There was a young girl of Detroit
Who at fucking was very adroit:
   She could squeeze her vagina
   To a pin-point, or finer,
Or open it out like a quoit.

And she had a friend named Durand
Whose cock could contract or expand.
   He could diddle a midge
   Or the arch of a bridge–
Their performance together was grand!

There was a young lady named Hall
Wore a newspaper dress to a ball.
   The dress caught on fire
   And burned her entire
Front page, sporting section, and all.

A disgusting young man named McGill
Made his neighbors exceedingly ill
   When they learned of his habits
   Involving white rabbits
And a bird with a flexible bill.

There was a young fellow from Leeds
Who swallowed a package of seeds.
    Great tufts of grass
    Sprouted out of his ass
And his balls were all covered with weeds.

There was a young girl whose divinity
Preserved her in perfect virginity.
    Till a candle, her nemesis,
    Caused parthenogenesis–
Now she thinks herself one of the Trinity.

In the reign of King George the Third,
The fashionable fuck was a bird:
    The hole of a sparrow
    Was dry, pink and narrow,
And was oiled with hummingbirds' turd.

There was a young lady named Nelly
Whose tits could be joggled like jelly.
    They could tickle her twat,
    Or be tied in a knot,
And could even swat flies on her belly.

"The testes are cooler outside,"
Said the doc to the curious bride.
   "For the semen must not
   Get too fucking hot,
And the bag fans your bum on the ride."

There was an old parson of Lundy,
Fell asleep in his vestry on Sunday.
   He awoke with a scream:
   "What, another wet dream!
That's what comes from not frigging since Monday."

Said Edna St. Vincent Millay
As she lay in the hay all asplay,
   "If you can make wine
   From these grapes, I opine,
We'll stay in this barn until May."

A chap down in Oklahoma
Had a cock that could sing *La Paloma,*
   But the sweetness of pitch
   Couldn't put off the hitch
Of impotence, size and aroma.

The grand-niece of Madame Du Barry
Suspected her son was a fairy.
"It's peculiar," said she,
"But he sits down to pee,
And stands when I bathe the canary."

A gentleman living in Fife
Made love to the corpse of his wife.
"How could I know, Judge?
She was cold, did not budge–
Just the same as she'd acted in life."

While pissing on deck, an old boatswain
Fell asleep, and his pisser got frozen.
It snapped at the shank
It fell off and sank
In the sea–'twas his own fault for dozin'!

When a girl, young Elizabeth Barrett
Was found by her Ma in a garret,
She had shoved up a diamond
As far as her hymen,
And was ramming it home with a carrot.

There was a young fellow of Mayence
Who fucked his own ass in defiance
   Not only of habit
   And morals but—damn it!—
Most of the known laws of science.

❧

There was a young lady of Cheam
Who crept into the vestry unseen.
   She pulled down her knickers,
   Likewise the vicar's
And said, "How about it, old bean?"

❧

"At a seance," said a young man named Post,
"I was being sucked off by a ghost;
   Someone switched on the lights
   And there in gauze tights,
On his knees, was Tobias mine host."

❧

In his garden remarked Lord Larkeeling:
"A fig for your digging and weeding.
   I like watching birds
   While they're dropping their turds,
And spying on guinea pigs breeding."

There was a young girl of Kilkenny
On whose genital parts there were many
   Venereal growths–
   The result of wild oats
Sown there by a fellow named Benny.

The modern cinematic emporium
Is not just a super-sensorium
   But a highly effectual
   Heterosexual
Mutual masturbatorium.

When Brother John wanted a screw
He would stuff a fat cat in a shoe,
   Pull up his cassock
   And kneel on a hassock
While doing his damnedest to mew.

"It's dull in Duluth, Minnesota,
Of spirit there's not an iota–"
   Complained Alice to Joe
   Who tried not to show
That he yawned in her snatch as he blowed her.

The Shah of the Empire of Persia
Lay for days in a sexual merger.
   When the nautch asked the Shah,
   "Won't you ever withdraw?"
He replied with a yawn, "It's inertia."

❦

There was a young curate of Eltham
Who wouldn't fuck girls, but he felt 'em.
   In lanes he would linger
   And play at stick-finger,
And scream with delight when he smelt 'em.

❦

A disciple of symbolist Jung,
Asked his wife, "May I bugger your bung?"
   And was so much annoyed
   When he found she read Freud,
He went out in the yard and ate dung.

❦

Said the Duchess of Danzer at tea,
"Young man, do you fart when you pee?"
   I replied with some wit,
   "Do you belch when you shit?"
I think that was one up for me.

A marine being sent to Hong Kong
Got a doctor to alter his dong.
He sailed off with a tool
Flat and thin as a rule–
When he got there he found he was wrong.

A finicky young whippersnapper
Had ways so revoltingly dapper
That a young lady's quim
Didn't interest him
If it hadn't a cellophane wrapper.

"Well, I took your advice," said McKnopp,
"And told the wife to get up on top.
She bounced about a bit,
Didn't quite get the hang of it,
And the kids, much amused, made us stop."

There was a young lady of Rheims
Who amazingly pissed four streams.
A friend poked around
And a fly-button found
Wedged tightly in one of her seams.

A geneticist living in Delft,
Scientifically played with himself;
When he was done
He labeled it: *Son,*
And filed him away on the shelf.

While fucking one night, Dr. Zuck
In his ears got his wife's nipples stuck.
With his thumb up her bum,
He could hear himself come–
This inventing the Telephone Fuck.

There was a young fellow named Howell
Who buggered himself with a trowel.
The triangular shape
Was conducive to rape,
And was easily cleaned with a towel.

There was a young man from Port Said
Who fell down a shit-house and died.
His unfortunate mother,
She fell down another;
And now they're interred side by side.

A gentle old Dame they called Muir
Had a mind so delightfully pure
  That she fainted away
  At a friend's house one day
When she saw some canary manure.

I dined with Lord Hughy Fitz-Bluing
Who said "Do you squirm when you're screwing?"
  I replied "Simple shagging
  Without any wagging
Is only for screwing canoeing."

There was a young man in Woods Hole
Who had an affair with a mole.
  Though a bit of a nancy
  He *did like* to fancy
Himself in the dominant role.

"Remind me, dear," said Sir Keith,
"As soon as I've brushed my teeth,
  To take down this glass
  And examine my ass
From behind–and of course from beneath."

A pious young lady named Finnegan
Would caution her friend, "Well, you're in again;
  So time it aright,
  Make it last through the night,
For I certainly don't want to sin again!"

A circus performer named Ditts
Was subject to passionate fits,
  But his pleasure in life
  Was to suck off his wife
As he swung by his knees from her tits.

Young girls who frequent picture-palaces
Are amused at the vogue of analysis,
  And giggle that Freud
  Should be less than annoyed
While they tickle contemporary phalluses.

A musical student from Sparta
Was a truly magnificent farter:
  On the strength of one bean
  He'd fart "God Save the Queen,"
And Beethoven's "Moonlight Sonata."

An avant-garde bard named McNamiter
Had a tool of enormous diameter.
But it wasn't the size
Brought tears to her eyes.
'Twas the rhythm–dactylic hexameter!

There was a young girl of Peru
Who had nothing whatever to do,
So she sat on the stairs
And counted cunt hairs–
Four thousand, three hundred, and two.

There was a young fellow of Eversham
Wrote a treatise on cunts and on sucking them.
But a lady from Wales
Took the wind from his sails
With an essay on ass-holes and fucking them.

"Now listen, young girl," said McPhett,
"You tell me your cunt is all wet.
Yet when I shove, you squirm,
Waste my boiling hot sperm–
You don't want to fuck, only sweat!"

Dr. John Donne, a Dean to St. Paul,
Grew old, and his prick rather small.
  Though he buggered a bug
  At the edge of a rug,
The insect scarce felt it at all.

❦

There once was a sailor from Wales,
An expert at pissing in gales.
  He could piss in a jar
  From the top-gallant spar
Without even wetting sails.

❦

Cleopatra, while helping to pump,
Ground out such a furious bump
  That Antony's dick
  Snapped off like a stick
And left him to pump with the stump.

❦

There once was a curate named Swope
Who wanted to bugger the Pope–
  To destroy the division
  Twixt his lust and religion
And, on the side, get an Archbishop's cope.

There was a young fellow named Lock
Who was born with a two-headed cock.
  When he'd fondle the thing
  It would rise up and sing
An antiphonal chorus by Bach.

But whether these two ever met
Has not been recorded as yet—
  Still, it would be diverting
  To see him inserting
His whang while it sang a duet!

In spite of a wasting disease
O'Reilly went down on his knees
  Before altars of gods,
  Whores, boys, and small dogs—
And all this for very small fees.

A piano composer named Liszt
Played with one hand while he pissed.
  But as he grew older
  His technique grew bolder,
And in concert jacked off with his fist.

There lives a young girl in New York
Who is cautious from fear of the stork.
   You will find she is taped
   To prevent being raped,
And her ass-hole is plugged with a cork.

In bed Dr. Oscar McPugh
Spoke of Spengler–and ate crackers too.
   His wife said, "Oh, stuff
   That philosophy guff
Up your ass, dear, and throw me a screw!"

A Sunday-School student in Mass.
Soon rose to the head of the class,
   By reciting quite bright
   And sleeping at night
With his tongue up the minister's ass.

While out on a picnic, McFee
Was stung on the balls by a bee.
   He made oodles of money
   By oozing pure honey
Every time he attempted to pee.

There was a young man of Bombay
Who fashioned a cunt out of clay.
  The heat of his prick
  Turned the damned thing to brick
And wore all his foreskin away.

To succeed in the brothels at Derna
One always begins as a learner.
  Indentured at six
  As a greaser of pricks,
One may rise to be fitter and turner.

There was a young lady whose joys
Were achieved with incomparable poise.
  She could have an orgasm
  With never a spasm–
She could fart without making a noise.

When Theocritus guarded his flock
He piped in the shade of a rock.
  It is said that his Muse
  Was one of the ewes
With a bum like a pink hollyhock.

There once was a son-of-a-bitch,
Neither clever, nor handsome, nor rich,
   Yet the girls he would dazzle,
   And fuck to a frazzle,
And then *ditch* them, the son-of-a-bitch!

❦

There was a young fellow named Blaine,
And he screwed some disgusting old jane.
   She was ugly and smelly,
   With an awful pot-belly,
But . . . well, they were caught in the rain.

❦

A middle-aged codger named Bruin
Found his love life completely a-ruin,
   For he flirted with flirts
   Wearing pants and no skirts,
And he never got in for no screwin'.

❦

There was a young man from Calcutta
Who was heard in his beard to mutter,
   "If her Bartholin glands
   Don't respond to my hands,
I'm afraid I shall have to use butter."

There once was a kiddie named Carr
Caught a man on top of his mar.
As he saw him stick 'er,
He said with a snicker,
"You do it much faster than par."

There once was a gouty old colonel
Who grew glum when the weather grew vernal,
And he cried in his tiffin
For his prick wouldn't stiffen,
And the *size* of the thing was infernal.

A lonely young lad of Eton
Used always to sleep with the heat on,
Till he ran into a lass
Who showed him her ass–
Now they sleep with only a sheet on.

A reckless young lady of France
Had no qualms about taking a chance,
But she thought it was crude
To get screwed in the nude,
So she always went home with damp pants.

Have you heard of knock-kneed Samuel McGuzzum
Who married Samantha, his bow-legged cousin?
   Some people say
   Love finds a way,
But for Sam and Samantha it doesn'.

❦

There was a young lady named May
Who strolled in a park by the way,
   And she met a young man
   Who fucked her and ran–
Now she goes to the park every day.

❦

There once was a Swede in Minneapolis,
Discovered his sex life was hapless:
   The more he would screw
   The more he'd want *to,*
And he feared he would soon be quite sapless.

❦

There was a young dolly named Molly
Who thought that to frig was folly.
   Said she, "You pee-pee
   Means nothing to me,
But I'll do it just to be jolly."

"I once knew a harlot named Lou–
And a versatile girl she was, too.
After ten years of whoredom
She perished of boredom
When she married a jackass like you!"

There was a young lady of Gloucester
Whose friends they thought they had lost her,
Till they found on the grass
The marks of her arse,
And the knees of the man who had crossed her.

Winter is here with his grouch,
The time when you sneeze and slouch.
You can't take you women
Canoein' or swimmin',
But a lot can be done on a couch.

A worn-out young husband named Lehr
Heard daily his wife's plaintive prayer:
"Slip on a sheath, quick,
Then slip your big dick
Between these lips covered with hair."

There was a young man of Ostend
Who let a girl play with his end.
   She took hold of Rover,
   And felt it all over,
And it did what she didn't intend.

There was a young man of Ostend
Whose wife caught him fucking her friend.
   "It's no use, my duck,
   Interrupting your fuck,
For I'm damned if I draw till I spend."

A newly-wed man of Peru
Found himself in a terrible stew:
   His wife was in bed
   Much deader than dead,
And so he had no one to screw.

His wife had a nice little cunt:
It was hairy, and soft, and in front,
   And with this she would fuck him,
   Though sometimes she'd suck him—
A charming, if commonplace, stunt.

I could hear the dull buzz of the bee
As he sunk his grub hooks into me.
  Her ass it was fine
  But you should have seen mine
In the shade of the old apple tree.

There was a young lady named Twiss
Who said she thought fucking a bliss,
  For it tickled her bum
  And caused her to come
While comfortably lying like this.

There was a young lady named Blount
Who had a rectangular cunt.
  She learned for diversion
  Posterior perversion,
Since no one could fit her in front.

There was a young lady named Brent
With a cunt of enormous extent,
  And so deep and so wide,
  The acoustics inside
Were so good you could hear when you spent.

There once was a Queen of Bulgaria
Whose bush had grown hairier and hairier,
  Till a Prince from Peru
  Who came up for a screw
Had to hunt for her cunt with a terrier.

❦

I met a young man in Chungking
Who had a very long thing–
  But you'll guess my surprise
  When I found that its size
Just measured a third-finger ring!

❦

There once was a girl from Cornell
Whose teats were shaped like a bell.
  When you touched them they shrunk,
  Except when she was drunk,
And then they got bigger than hell.

❦

There was a young lady whose cunt
Could accommodate a small punt.
  Her mother said, "Annie,
  It matches your fanny,
Which never was that of a runt."

There was a young man from East Wubley
Whose cock was bifurcated doubly.
   Each quadruplicate shaft
   Had two balls hanging aft,
And the general effect was quite lovely.

There was a young fellow of Greenwich
Whose balls were all covered with spinach.
   He had such a tool
   It was wound on a spool,
And he reeled it out inich by inich.

But this tale has an unhappy finich,
For due to the sand in the spinach
   His ballocks grew rough
   And wrecked his wife's muff,
And scratched up her thatch in the scrimmage.

There was a young fellow of Harrow
Whose john was the size of a marrow.
   He said to his tart,
   "How's this for a start?
My balls are outside in a barrow."

There was a young girl named Heather
Whose twitcher was made out of leather.
   She made a queer noise,
   Which attracted the boys,
By flapping the edges together.

Oh, pity the Duchess of Kent!
Her cunt is so dreadfully bent,
   The poor wench doth stammer,
   "I need a sledgehammer
To pound a man into my vent."

A contortionist hailing from Lynch
Used to rent out his tool by the inch.
   A foot cost a quid–
   He could and he did
Stretch it to three in a pinch.

A farmer I know named O'Doole
Has a long and incredible tool.
   He can used it to plow,
   Or to diddle a cow,
Or just as a cue-stick at pool.

When I was a baby, my penis
Was as white as the buttocks of Venus.
   But now 'tis as red
   As her nipples instead–
All because of the feminine genus!

A very odd pair are the Pitts:
His balls are as large as her tits,
   Her tits are as large
   As an invasion barge–
Neither knows how the other cohabits.

A beautiful lady named Psyche
Is loved by a fellow named Ikey.
   One thing about Ike
   The lady can't like
Is his prick, which is dreadfully spikey.

There was a young harlot named Schwartz
Whose cock-pit was studded with warts,
   And they tickled so nice
   She drew a high price
From the studs at the summer resorts.

There was a young lady named Astor
Who never let any get past her.
She finally got plenty
By stopping at twenty,
Which certainly ought to last her.

There was an old man of Cajon
Who never could get a good bone.
With the aid of a gland
It grew simply grand;
Now his wife cannot leave it alone.

There once was a lady named Carter,
Fell in love with a virile young Tartar.
She stripped off his pants,
At his prick quickly glanced,
And cried: "For that I'll be a martyr!"

There was a young man with a fiddle
Who asked of his girl, "Do you diddle?"
She replied, "Yes, I do,
But prefer to with two–
It's twice as much fun in the middle."

There was a young fellow named Fletcher,
Was reputed an infamous lecher.
  When he'd take on a whore
  She'd need a rebore,
And they'd carry him out on a stretcher.

I know of a fortunate Hindu
Who is sought in the towns that he's been to
  By the ladies he knows,
  Who are thrilled to the toes
By the tricks he can make his foreskin do.

There was a young miss from Johore
Who'd lie on a mat on the floor;
  In a manner uncanny
  She'd wobble her fanny,
And drain your nuts dry to the core.

There was a young lady named Mable
Who liked to sprawl out on the table,
  Then cry to her man,
  "Stuff in all you can–
Get your ballocks in, too, if you're able."

There was a young lady named Nance
Who learned about fucking in France,
And when you'd insert it
She'd squeeze till she hurt it,
And shoved it right back in your pants.

There was a young girl named O'Clare
Whose body was covered with hair.
It was really quite fun
To probe with one's gun,
For her quimmy might be anywhere.

While spending the winter at Pau
Lady Pamela forgot to say "No."
So the head-porter made her
The second-cook laid her;
The waiters were all hanging low.

'Tis said that the Emperor Titius
Had a penchant for pleasantries vicious.
He took two of his nieces
And fucked them to pieces,
And said it was simply delicious.

There was a young man from Toledo
Who was cursed with excessive libido.
To fuck and to screw,
And to fornicate too,
Were the three major points of his credo.

A virile young man of Touraine.
Had vesicles no one could drain.
With an unbroken flow
Thrice the course he would go,
Then roll over and start in again.

A young man with a passion quite vast
Used to talk about making it last,
Till one day he discovered
His sister uncovered,
And now he fucks often–and fast.

There was a young fellow from Wark
Who, when he screws, has to bark.
His wife is a bitch
With a terrible itch,
So the town never sleeps after dark.

There was a young girl of Samoa
Who plugged up her cunt with a boa.
  This strange contraceptive
  Was very deceptive
To all but the spermatozoa.

There's an over-sexed lady named Whyte
Who insists on a dozen a night.
  A fellow named Cheddar
  Had the brashness to wed her—
His chance of survival is slight.

Said a man to a maid of Ashanti,
"Can one sniff of your twitchet, or can't he?"
  Said she with a grin,
  "Sure, shove your nose in!
But *presto,* please—not too *andante.*"

There was a young lass of Blackheath
Who frigged an old man with her teeth.
  She complained that he stunk
  Not so much from the spunk,
But his arsehole was just underneath.

A girl with a sebaceous cyst
Always came when her asshole was kissed.
  Her lover was gratified
  That she was so satisfied,
But regretted the fun that he missed.

There once was a maid in Duluth,
A striver and seeker of truth.
  This pretty wench
  Was adept at French,
And said all else was uncouth.

There was a young lady named Hix
Who was fond of sucking big pricks.
  One fellow she took
  Was a doctor named Snook,
Now *he's* in a hell of a fix.

There was a young lady named Grace
Who took all she could in her face,
  But an adequate lad
  Gave her all that he had,
And blew tonsils all over the place.

The priests at the temple of Isis
Used to offer up amber and spices,
   Then back of the shrine
   They would play 69
And other unmentionable vices.

❦

A Roman of old named Horatio
Was fond of a form of fellatio.
   He kept accurate track
   Of the boys he'd attack,
And called it his cock-sucking ratio.

❦

There was an old maid from Luck
Who took it into her head to fuck.
   She was about to resign
   Till she hung out a sign:
"Come in, I've decided to suck."

❦

There was a young bounder named Link
Who possessed a very tart dink.
   To sweeten it some
   He steeped it in rum,
And he's driven the ladies to drink.

Said the priest to Miss Bridget McLennin,
"Sure, a kiss of your twat isn't sinnin'."
And he stuck to this story
Till he tasted the gory
And menstruous state she was then in.

A socialite out on Nantucket
Had a twat that was wide as a bucket.
She proclaimed, "If it's clean
I will take it between–
If it's rotten I'd far better suck it."

An old doctor who lacked protoplasm
Tried to give his young wife an orgasm,
But his tongue jumped the track
'Twixt the front and the back.
And got pinched in a bad anal spasm.

Old Louis Quatorze was hot stuff.
He tired of that game, blindman's buff,
Up-ended his mistress,
Kissed hers while she kissed his,
And thus taught the world *soixante-neuf.*

There's a dowager near Sweden Landing
Whose manners are odd and demanding.
   It's one of her jests
   To suck off her guests—
She hates to keep gentlemen standing.

There was a young fellow named Taylor
Who seduced a respectable sailor.
   When they put him in jail
   He worked out the bail
By licking the parts of the jailer.

Have you heard of young Franchot Tone,
Who felt of his own peculiar bone?
   It was long and quite narrow
   And filled full of marrow,
And less edible than stale corn pone.

There was an old lady of Troy
Who invented a new kind of joy:
   She sugared her quim,
   And frosted the rim,
And then had it sucked by a boy.

A young man who lived in Balbriggan
Went to sea to recover from frigging,
But after a week
As they climbed the fore-peak
He buggered the mate in the rigging.

Some night when you're drunk on Dutch Bols
Try changing the usual rôles.
The backward position
Is nice for coition
And it offers the choice of two holes.

There was a young man from Chubut
Who had a remarkable root:
When hard it would bend
With a curve at the end,
So he fucked himself in the petoot.

When she wanted a new way to futter
He greased her behind with butter;
Then, with a sock,
In went his jock,
And they carried her home on a shutter.

A Sultan of old Istamboul
Had a varicose vein in his tool.
   This evoked joyous grunts
   From his harem of cunts,
But his boys suffered pain at the stool.

There was a young fellow named Kelly
Who preferred his wife's ass to her belly.
   He shrieked with delight
   As he ploughed through the shite,
And filled up her hole with his jelly.

There was a young mate of a lugger
Who took out a girl just to hug her.
   "I've my monthlies," she said,
   "And a cold in the head,
But my bowels work well . . . Do you bugger?"

There was a young lady whose mind
Was never especially refined.
   She got on her knees,
   Her lover to please,
Who stuck in his prick from behind.

There was a young man from Nantasket
Who screwed a dead whore in a casket.
He allowed 'twas no vice,
But thought it was nice,
For she needed no money, nor'd ask it.

A phenomenal fellow named Preston
Has a hair-padded lower intestine.
Though exceedingly fine
In the buggery line,
It isn't much good for digestin'.

A modern monk nicknamed Augustin,
His penis a boy's bottom thrust in.
Then said Father Ignatius,
"Now really! Good gracious!
Your conduct is really disgusting."

There was a young Bishop from Brest
Who openly practiced incest.
"My sisters and nieces
Are all dandy pieces,
And they don't cost a cent," he confessed.

I once had the wife of a Dean
Seven times while the Dean was out ski'in'.
   She remarked with some gaiety,
   "Not bad for the laity,
Though the Bishop once managed thirteen."

There was a young monk from Dundee
Who hung a nun's cunt on a tree.
   He grabbed her fair ass
   And performed a high mass
That even the Pope came to see.

A rooster residing in Spain
Used to diddle his hens in the rain.
   "I give them a bloody
   Good time when it's muddy:
Which keeps them from getting too vain."

There was a young lady named Sutton
Who said, as she carved up the mutton,
   "My father preferred
   The last sheep in the herd–
This is one of his children I'm cuttin'."

There was a young lady of Wohl's Hill
Who sat herself down on a mole's hill.
  The resident mole
  Stuck his head up her hole–
The lady's all right, but the mole's ill.

There was a young man of Bhogat,
The cheeks of whose ass were so fat
  That they had to be parted
  Whenever he farted,
And propped wide apart when he shat.

There was a young lady of Dexter
Whose husband exceedingly vexed her,
  For whenever they'd start
  He'd unfailingly fart
With a blast that damn nearly unsexed her.

There was a young woman named Dottie
Who said as she sat on her potty,
  "It isn't polite
  To do this in sight,
But then, who am I to be snotty?"

There was a young fellow of Ealing,
Devoid of all delicate feeling.
When he read on the door:
"Don't shit on the floor"
He jumped up and shat on the ceiling.

❧

There was a young virgin of Bude
Whose tricks, thought exciting, were viewed
With distrust by the males
For she'd fondle their rails,
But never would let them intrude.

❧

There was an old spinster named Campbell
Got tangled one day in a bramble.
She cried, "Ouch, how it sticks!
But so many sharp pricks
Are not met every day on a ramble."

❧

There was a young virgin of Dover
Who was raped in the woods by a drover.
When the going got hard
He greased her with lard,
Which felt nice, so they started all over.

There was a bluestocking in Florence
Wrote anti-sex pamphlets in torrents,
Till a Spanish grandee
Got her off with his knee,
And she burned all her works with abhorrence.

A neuropath-virgin named Flynn
Shouted before she gave in:
"It isn't the deed,
Or the fear of the seed,
But that big worm that's shedding its skin!"

There were three young ladies of Grimsby
Who said, "Of what use can our quims be?
The hole in the middle
Is so we can piddle,
But for what can the hole in the rims be?"

There was a young girl from Hoboken
Who claimed that her hymen was broken
From riding a bike
On a cobblestone pike,
But it really was broken from pokin'.

A lady of virginal humours
Would only be screwed through her bloomers.
  But one fatal day
  The bloomers gave way,
Which fixed her for future consumers.

❧

No one can tell about Myrtle
Whether she's sterile or fertile.
  If anyone tries
  To tickle her thighs
She closes them tight like a turtle.

❧

A Newfoundland lad from Placentia
Was in love to the point of dementia,
  But his love couldn't burgeon
  With his touch-me-not virgin
'Til he screwed her by hand in absentia.

❧

There was a young lady from 'Quoddie
Who had a magnificent body,
  And her face was not bad,
  Yet she's never been had
For her odor was markèdly coddy.

A pathetic appellant at Reno
Was as chaste as the holy Bambino,
   For she'd married a slicker
   Who stuck to his liquor
And scorned her ripe maraschino.

There was an old spinster of Tyre
Who bellowed, "My cunt is on fire!"
   So a fireman was found,
   Brought his engine around,
And extinguished her burning desire.

There was a young lady of Worcester
Who dreamt that a rooster seduced her.
   She woke with a scream,
   But 'twas only a dream–
A bump in the mattress had goosed her.

There was a young lady of France
Who went to the Palace to dance.
   She danced with a Turk
   Till he got in his dirk,
And now she can't button her pants.

A medical student named Hetrick
Is learnèd in matters obstetric.
From a glance at the toes
Of the mother, he knows
If the fetus's balls are symmetric.

❦

There was a young lady of Maine
Who declared she'd a man on the brain.
But you knew from the view
Of the way her waist grew,
It was not on her brain that he'd lain.

❦

There was an old whore of Marseilles
Who tried the new rotary spray.
Said she, "Ah, that's better . . .
Why here's a French letter
That's been missing since Armistice Day!"

❦

There was an old whore of Algiers
Who had bushels of dirt in her ears.
The tip of her titty
Was also quite shitty.
She never had washed it in years.

A young man, quite free with his dong,
Said the thing could be had for a song.
  Such response did he get
  That he rented the Met,
And held auditions all the day long.

A sempstress at Epping-on-Tyne
Used to peddle her tail down the line.
  She first got a crown,
  But her prices went down–
Now she'll fit you for ten pence or nine.

There was a young lady of Erskine,
And the chief of her charms was her fair skin,
  But the sable she wore
  (She had several more)
She had earned while wearing her bare skin.

A shiftless young fellow of Kent
Had his wife fuck the landlord for rent.
  But as she grew older
  The landlord grew colder,
And now they live out in a tent.

Any whore whose door sports a red light
Knows a prick when she sees one, all right.
   She can tell by a glance
   At the drape of men's pants
If they're worth taking on for the night.

❧

There was a young lady named Mable
Who would fuck on a bed or a table.
   Though a two-dollar screw
   Was the best she could do,
Her ass bore a ten-dollar label.

❧

Said a naked young soldier named Mickey
As his cunt eyed his stiff, throbbing dickey,
   "Kid, my leave's almost up,
   But I feel like a tup;
Bend down, and I'll slip you a quickie."

❧

A school marm from old Mississippi
Had a quim that was simply zippy.
   The scholars all praised it
   Till finally she raised it
To prices befitting a chippy.

There was a young thing from Missouri
Who fancied herself as a houri.
   Her friends thus forsook her,
   For a harlot they took her,
And she gave up the role in a fury.

There was a young lady named Moore
Who, while not quite precisely a whore,
   Couldn't pass up a chance
   To take down her pants,
And compare some man's stroke with her bore.

A tired young trollop of Nome
Was worn out from her toes to her dome.
   Eight miners came screwing,
   But she said, "Nothing doing;
One of you has to go home!"

A chippy whose name was O'Dare
Sailed on a ship to Kenmare,
   But this cute little honey
   Had left home her money
So she laid the whole crew for her fare.

Says a busy young whore named Miss Randalls,
As men by the dozens she handles,
"When I get this busy
My cunt gets all jizzy,
And it runs down my legs like wax candles."

❦

There was a young lady in Reno
Who lost all her dough playing keeno.
But she lay on her back
And opened her crack,
And now she owns the casino.

❦

There was an old girl of Silesia
Who said, "As my cunt doesn't please ya,
You might as well come
Up my slimy old bum,
But be careful my tapeworm don't seize ya."

❦

There was a young whore from Tashkent
Who managed an immoral tent.
Day out and day in
She lay writhing in sin,
Giving thanks it was ten months to Lent.

There once was a knowledgeful whore
Who knew all the coital lore.
  But she found there were many
  Who preferred her fat fanny,
And now she don't fuck any more.

There once was a versatile whore,
As expert behind as before.
  For a quid you could view her,
  And bugger and screw her,
As she stood on her head on the floor.

There was a young fellow–a banker,
Had bubo, itch, pox, and chancre.
  He got all the four
  From the dirty old whore,
So he wrote her a letter to thank her.

There was a young man of Back Bay
Who thought syphilis just went away,
  And felt that a chancre
  Was merely a canker
Acquired in lascivious play.

There was an old man of Goditch,
Had the syph and the clap and the itch.
  His name was McNabs
  And he also had crabs,
The dirty old son of a bitch.

An explorer returned from Australia,
Reported lost paraphernalia:
  A Zeiss microscope
  And his personal hope,
Which had vanished with his genitalia.

There was an old maid from Bermuda
Who shot a marauding intruder.
  It was not her ire
  At his lack of attire,
But he reached for her jewels as he screwed her.

A miner who bored in Brazil
Found some very strange rust on his drill.
  He thought it a joke
  Till the bloody thing broke–
Now his tailings are practically nil.

An eccentric young poet named Brown
Raised up his embroidered gown
  To look for his peter
  To beat it to metre,
But fainted when none could be found.

The wife of a red-headed Celt
Lost the key to her chastity-belt.
  She tried picking the lock
  With an Ulsterman's cock,
And the next thing he knew, he was gelt.

The wife of an athlete named Chuck
Found her married life shit-out-of-luck.
  Her husband played hockey
  Without wearing a jockey–
Now he hasn't got what it takes for a fuck.

There was a young girl from the Creek
Who had her periods twice every week.
  "How very provoking,"
  Said the Vicar from Woling,
"There's no time for poking, so to speak."

The wife of a chronic crusader
Took on every man who waylaid her.
   Till the amorous itch
   Of this popular bitch
So annoyed the crusader he spayed her.

There was a young fellow named Nick
Who was cursed with a spiralling prick.
   So he set out to hunt
   For a screw-twisted cunt
That would match with his corkscrewy dick.

He found one, and took it to bed,
And then in chagrin he dropped dead,
   For that spiralling snatch
   It never would match–
The damn thing had a left-handed thread!

A gallant young Frenchman named Grandhomme
Was attempting a girl on a tandem.
   At the height of the make
   She slammed on the brake,
And scattered his semen at random.

There was an old sheik named Al Hassid
Whose tool had become very placid.
   Before each injection
   To get an erection
He had to immerse it in acid.

Said old Mr. Wellington Koo,
"Now what in the Hell shall I do?
   My wife is too hot,
   I can't fill up her slot—"
So he screwed her to bits trying to.

A crooner who lived in Lahore
Got his balls caught in a door.
   Now his mezzo soprano
   Is rather piano
Though he was a loud basso before.

There was a young man of Bagdad
Who was dreaming that he was a shad.
   He dreamt he was spawning,
   And then, the next morning,
He found that, by Jesus! he had.

An eunuch frequenting Bangkok
Used to borrow the deified jock
From a local rain-god
When he went for a prod–
You could hear the girl yell for a block.

There was a young naval cadet
Whose dreams were unusually wet.
When he dreamt of his wedding
He soaked up the bedding,
And the wedding ain't taken place yet.

There was a gay Countess of Dufferin,
One night while her husband was covering,
Just to chaff him a bit
She said, "You old shit,
I can buy a dildo for a sovereign."

As Apollo was chasing the fair
Daphne she vanished in air.
He could find but a shrub
With thick bark on the hub
And not even a knot-hole to spare.

There were three young ladies of Fetters,
Annoyed all their elders and betters
By stuffing their cock-holders
With proxies for stockholders,
Old bills, and anonymous letters.

There was a young parson of Goring
Who made a small hole in the flooring.
He lined it all round,
Then laid on the ground,
And declared it was cheaper than whoring.

A vicious old whore of Albania
Hated men with a terrible mania.
With a twitch and a squirm
She would hold back your sperm,
And then roll on her face and disdain ya.

There was a young man of Kutki
Who could blink himself off with one eye.
For a while though, he pined,
When his organ declined
To function, because of a stye.

An innocent boy in Lapland
Was told that frigging was grand.
But at his first trial
He said with a smile,
"I've had the same feeling by hand."

There is a young fellow from Leeds
Whose skin is so thin his cock bleeds
Whenever erect;
This dermal defect
Often scares him from sowing his seeds.

There was a young fellow from Lees
Who handled his tool with great ease.
This continual friction
Made his sex a mere fiction,
But the callus hangs down to his knees.

There was a young man from McGill
Who was always seen walking uphill.
When someone inquired,
"My man, aren't you tired?"
He said, "No, it makes my balls thrill."

There was a young man named M'Gurk
Who dozed off one night after work.
He had a wet dream
But awoke with a scream
Just in time to give it a jerk.

There was a young lady named May
Who frigged herself in the hay.
She bought a pickle–
One for a nickel–
And wore all the warts away!

A nymphomaniacal nurse
With a curse that was worse than perverse
Stuck a rotary drill
Up her twat, for a thrill–
And they carted her off in a hearse.

A eunuch who came from Port Said
Had a jolly good time in bed,
Nor could any sultana
Detect from his manner
That he used a banana instead.

A reformer who went out to Bali
To change the sartorial folly
Of the girls now admits,
"A pair of good tits
In season can seem rather jolly."

There was a young Queen of Baroda
Who built a new kind of pagoda.
The walls of its halls
Were festooned with the balls
And the tools of the fools that bestrode her.

There was a young lady in Brent,
When her old man's pecker it bent,
She said with a sigh,
"Oh, why must it die?
Let's fill it with Portland Cement."

There was an old man from Bubungi
Whose balls were all covered with fungi.
With his friends, out at lunch,
He tore off a bunch
And said, "Now divide this among ye."

A mystical painter named Foxx
Once picked up a girl on the docks.
He made an elliptic
Mysterious triptych,
And painted it right on her box.

There was a young cowboy named Gary
Who was morbidly anxious to marry,
But he found the defection
Of any erection
A difficult factor to parry.

A young baseball-fan named Miss Glend
Was the home-team's best rooter and friend.
But for her the big league
Never held the intrigue
Of a bat with two balls at the end.

The favorite pastime of grandfather
Was tickling his balls with a feather.
But the thing he liked best
Of all the rest
Was knocking them gently together.

There was a young man named Ignatius
Who lived in a garret quite spacious.
When he went to his auntie's
He always wore panties,
But alone in his garret—good gracious!

❦

There is a young nurse in Japan
Who lifts men by their pricks to the pan.
A trick of jujitsu,
And either it shits you
Or makes you feel more like a man.

❦

The prick of a young man of Kew
Showed veins that were azure of hue.
Its head was quite red
So he waved it and said,
"Three cheers for the red, white, and blue."

❦

A clever inventory named Krupp
Wore a belt when he wanted to tup.
His mighty dry cells
Made her tits buzz like bells,
And lighted the hall-entrance up.

Quoth the coroner's jury in Preston,
"The verdict is rectal congestion."
  They found an eight-ball
  On a shoemaker's awl
Halfway up the major's intestine.

There was a young lady of Asia
Who had an odd kind of aphasia.
  She'd forget that her cunt
  Was located in front,
Which deprived her of most of the pleasure.

There was a young girl of Asturias
With a penchant for practices curious.
  She loved to bat rocks
  With her gentlemen's cocks–
A practice both rude and injurious.

A lecherous fellow named Babbitt
Asked a girl if she'd fuck or would nab it.
  Said she, "From long habit
  I fuck like a rabbit,
So I'd rather cohabit than grab it."

The ancient orthographer, Chisholm,
Caused a lexicographical schism
   When he asked to know whether
   'Twere known which was better
To use–*g* or *j*–to spell *jism.*

The Duchess of Drood's lewd and crude,
And the men think her terribly rude.
   When they swim by the docks
   She tickles their cocks
And laughs when the red tips protrude.

A certain young lady named Daisy
Who is really infernally lazy
   Said, "I haven't the time
   To wipe my behine,
But the way I can hump drives 'em crazy."

A surly and pessimist Druid,
A defeatist, if only he knew it,
   Said, "The world's on the skids,
   And I think having kids
Is a waste of good seminal fluid."

A company of Grenadier Guards
While traversing the park, formed in squads,
   Saw two naked statues
   At three-quarter pratt views,
Which perceptibly stiffened their rods.

❦

There was a young athlete named Grimmon
Who developed a new way of swimmin':
   By a marvellous trick
   He would scull with his prick,
Which attracted loud cheers from the women.

❦

There once was a lady hand-letterer
Who thought of a program to better her.
   She hand-lettered each
   Of the parts she could reach,
The bosoms, the navel, et cetera.

❦

An ingenious young fellow named Herman
Tied a bow on the end of his worm, and
   His wife said, "How festive!"
   But he said, "Don't be restive–
You'll wriggle it off with your squirmin'."

When Angelico worked in cerise,
For the angel he painted his niece.
  In a heavenly trance
  He pulled off her pants,
And erected a fine altar-piece.

A mason, one of the Malones
Put a coat of cement on his stones.
  "They keep warmer at night,
  And are bound to hang tight,
And not bruise themselves on my knee-bones."

There was an eccentric from Mecca
Who discovered a record from Decca,
  Which he twirled on his thumb
  (Those eccentrics are dumb)
While he needled the disc with his pecca.

A musicienne in gay Montebello
Amused herself playing the cello,
  But not a solo,
  For she used as a bow
The dong of a sturdy young fellow.

A bather whose clothing was strewed
By the winds that left her quite nude,
Saw a man come along,
And unless we are wrong
You expected this line to be lewd.

❧

The dong of a fellow named Grable
Was as pliant and long as a cable.
Each night while he ate,
This confirmed reprobate
Would screw his wife under the table.

❧

There was a young man from Peru
Whose lineage was noble all through.
Now this isn't crud,
For not only his blood
But even his semen was blue.

❧

There was a young man from Saskatchewan
Whose pecker was truly gargantuan.
It was good for large whores
And small dinosaurs,
And sufficiently rough to scratch a match upon.

There was a young man named Murray
Who made love to his girl in a surrey.
She started to sigh
But someone walked by,
So he buttoned his pants in a hurry.

❦

A young man whose sight was myopic
Thought sex an incredible topic.
So poor were his eyes,
That despite its great size,
His penis appeared microscopic.

❦

There was a young man named O'Neill,
Used to play on the old Campanile.
He made the gong bong
With the end of his dong–
Now he's trying to get it to heal.

❦

A prudish young damsel named Rose
Is particular how men propose.
To "Let's have intercourse,"
She says gaily, "Of course,"
But to "Let's fuck," she turns up her nose.

Said a certain sweet red-headed siren,
"Young sailors are cute—I must try one!"
She came home in the nude,
Stewed, screwed, and tattooed
With lewd pictures and verses from Byron.

❧

There was a young man up in Utah
Who constructed a cundum of pewter.
He said, "I confess
You feel nothing or less,
But it makes you as safe as a neuter."

❧

A fanatic gun-lover named Crust
Was perverse to the point of disgust.
His idea of a peach
Had a sixteen-inch breech,
And a pearl-handled 44 bust.

❧

A daring young maid from Dubuque
Risked a rather decided rebuke
By receiving a prude
In the absolute nude,
But he gasped, "IF you only could cook!"

If Leo your own birthday marks
You will fuck until 40, when starts
  A new pleasure in stamps,
  Boy Scouts and their camps,
And fondling nude statues in parks.

❦

There was a young blade from South Greece
Whose bush did so greatly increase
  That before he could shack
  He must hunt needle in stack.
'Twas as bad as being obese.

❦

There once was a gay young Parisian
Who screwed an appendix incision,
  And the girl of his choice
  Could hardly rejoice
At this horrible lack of precision.

❦

There once was a cuntlapper's daughter
Who, despite all her father had taught her,
  Would become so unstrung
  At the touch of a tongue
That she'd deluge her beau with her water.